北语对外汉语精版教材

速成汉语基础教程

Chinese Crash Course (Third Edition)

主　编：杨惠元

副主编：李德钧　韩　梅　游锋华

Integrated Textbook

综合课本（第3版）

6

北京语言大学出版社
BEIJING LANGUAGE AND CULTURE UNIVERSITY PRESS

图书在版编目（CIP）数据

速成汉语基础教程：综合课本. 6 / 杨惠元主编
. —3版. —北京：北京语言大学出版社, 2021.11
北语对外汉语精版教材
ISBN 978-7-5619-6019-6

Ⅰ. ①速… Ⅱ. ①杨… Ⅲ. ①汉语—对外汉语教学—教材 Ⅳ. ①H195.4

中国版本图书馆CIP数据核字（2021）第220652号

速成汉语基础教程 · 综合课本 6（第 3 版）
SUCHENG HANYU JICHU JIAOCHENG · ZONGHE KEBEN 6 (DI 3 BAN)

排版制作：华伦图文制作中心
责任印制：周 燚

出版发行：北京语言大学出版社
社　　址：北京市海淀区学院路 15 号，100083
网　　址：www.blcup.com
电子信箱：service@blcup.com
电　　话：编辑部　8610-82303395
　　　　　发行部　8610-82303650/3591/3648
　　　　　北语书店　8610-82303653
　　　　　网购咨询　8610-82303908
印　　刷：北京印迪数码科技有限公司

版　　次：1996 年 1 月第 1 版　2007 年 9 月第 2 版　2021 年 11 月第 3 版
印　　次：2021 年 11 月第 1 次印刷
开　　本：787 毫米 × 1092 毫米　1/16　　印　　张：13
字　　数：165 千字
定　　价：68.00 元

PRINTED IN CHINA

第3版前言

《速成汉语基础教程·综合课本》（第3版）是《速成汉语初级教程·综合课本》（北京语言文化大学出版社，1996）和《速成汉语基础教程·综合课本》（北京大学出版社，2007）的修订版。在修订过程中，我们努力保持原教材的优势和特色：

1. 全套8册共出词语3600多个，基本涵盖了外国留学生在中国学习、生活的常用词汇。因此，学习本教程的学生可提高使用汉语进行实际交际的能力。

2. 课文内容实用有趣，学生爱学、易学。原版教材筛选和安排了贴近学生生活的、学了就能用的话题，这样的内容学生喜欢学、愿意学。大部分课文语言风趣幽默，能够引起学生的学习兴趣，激发他们的学习积极性。

3. 语法点的讲解基本采用归纳法。由于课文编写不受语法点的绝对限制，允许冒出新的语法点，所以编写的课文语言自然、流畅。多年的教学经验证明，我们对成人的汉语教学，应先使他们对语言现象有真切的感性认识，然后到一定阶段再进行归纳总结，帮助他们上升到理性认识，这样做符合第二语言教学的规律。

4. 第3版的练习保持了前两版"语音 → 词语 → 句型 → 功能 → 成段表达 → 篇章结构 → 阅读理解"一条龙的练习模式。练习大多紧紧围绕当课的生词、课文和语法点，针对当课的重点和难点，为教师组织课堂教学以及对学生进行语言技能乃至语言交际技能的训练服务。

在广泛征求教材使用者意见的基础上，我们进行了修订，使教材进一步完善。我们替换了内容过时的课文，删去了不常用的生词，增加了使用频率高的新词。为方便教学，我们增加了一些练习，把原有的练习调整为课堂练习和家庭作业两个部分，这样课上课下既分工又合作。我们以课堂练习为主，家庭作业为辅。家庭作业既可以是课堂教学的弹性内容，也可以作为第二天课上复习、检查的内容。

修订这套教材，我们总的指导思想是：以语音、词汇、语法、汉字等语言要素的教学为基础，通过课堂教学，帮助学生把语言要素转化为语言技能，进而转化为语言交际技能。为此，我们提出以下教学建议：

1. 语音是学生语言能力的门面，也是对外汉语教学的难点之一，所以我们保留了语音集中教学的前10课，在其他各课中仍然进行分散的语音训练，希望教师根据学生的发音问题，有选择、有重点、有针对性地进行语音训练。特别是声调的练习，我们特意将“定调音节”的练习延伸到第四册。因为汉语词大部分是双音节词，掌握了双音节的声调，就等于掌握了大部分汉语词的声调。双音节声调搭配总共只有20个，我们选了20个双音节作为定调标准。掌握了这20个双音节的声调，以后学生出现声调错误时，用定调音节提示一下，他们便可自行改正。练习中的“朗读定调音节”在第一册前9课是朗读拼音，第一册第十课以后过渡为朗读汉字。

2. 第一册的重点虽然是语音训练，但教师在突出听说训练的同时，也要重视汉字的认读和书写练习，帮助学生打好汉字基础。第一、二册各课后都附有“汉字表”，为了简明，我们删去了“繁体”一栏（如有必要，另出版繁体字版），保留了笔画笔顺和构成合体字的拆分部件两个部分。

3. 第二册到第八册的重点是词语教学，教师要帮助学生全面掌握好词语的“音、形、义、用”。每课生词表里的生词包括课文中的生词和练习中的生词。按照北语的教学模式，教师应该要求学生课前预习好生词，基本掌握词语的“音”和“义”。课堂练习的重点是词语的“音、义、用”，特别是词语的搭配和活用。词语的“形”可让学生通过家庭作业掌握。

4. 离合词是汉语特有的语言现象，且大多是动词。在前两版中，有的作为词组处理，不标注词性，汉语拼音分写；有的作为词处理，标注动词，汉语拼音连写。本次修订统一作为词，标注词性，汉语拼音连写。因为特殊，学生难于掌握，常常用错，所以在教学中教师要重视离合词的讲练。

5. 本教程是为外国留学生编写的，生词表中有个别生词的拼音标的是变调

（包括轻声），而没有采用《现代汉语词典》（第7版）标注的本调。这样，他们学习和使用起来比较贴近生活。离合词的拼音连写也是基于这一理念。

6. 汉语普通话是以北京语音为标准音，以北方话为基础方言的。我们本着这一原则处理儿化音，根据北京语音在需要儿化的词语后都加了“儿”，以方便学生学习地道的汉语普通话。

7. 语法讲解从结构入手，不追求系统性，力求简单明白，重视语义和语用功能的说明。教师可通过图片、动作、视频等各种直观手段展示语法点，再进行机械练习，最后落实到活用上，使学生置身于语言交际情境中，而不是语法术语和概念中。

8. 课文以话题为中心，为学生提供交际的模式。第一册到第四册的重点是关于学习、生活方面的交际，从第五册开始，话题逐渐向社会交际过渡，增加介绍中国国情、中国人的观念习俗等文化方面的内容。教师要尽量引导学生以课文为范本，说他们自己想说而不会说的话，以此训练学生的汉语思维能力，开发他们的语言潜能，提高交际能力。

9. 本教程逢五逢十的课设计了“功能会话”练习，意在突出“结构与功能相结合”的原则。“功能会话”练习与当课关系不是很紧密，但有一定的概括性。

10. 教师可多采用任务教学法，给学生布置各种交际任务，多组织课堂活动，要求学生使用语言完成交际任务，在交际中学习语言，强化他们学习语言的成就感，激发他们的学习积极性。

编　者

2021年3月

Preface for the Third Edition

Chinese Crash Course: Integrated Textbook (Third Edition) is the revised version of the first edition (*Short Term Intensive Elementary Chinese*, 1996, Beijing Language and Culture University Press) and the second edition (*Speed-up Chinese: Integrated Textbook*, 2007, Peking University Press). It is with the following advantages and features reserved:

1. With a vocabulary over 3,600, the textbooks cover the useful and common vocabulary for foreign students to study and live in China. After learning this course, students are expected to improve their language proficiency in Chinese communication.

2. The materials we used are student-centered, practical and interesting. The unrevised version provided students with materials from daily life, which can be put into practice immediately after class. The language of texts has a fine sense of humor, in which we believe students would be highly motivated in their language acquisition.

3. We apply inductive method to elaborate the grammar points. We have briefly dealt with the most frequently used grammatical rules and explained them in as non-technical a way as possible. New grammar points are not strictly confined to certain text since long-year teaching experience shows that for adult-learners, a general impression for the language will help them form a stronger foundation for their language learning.

4. The training mode of "pronunciation→words and phrases→sentence patterns→function→expressions in paragraph→discourse structure→reading comprehension" keeps unchanged in the third edition. The exercises are closely related to the text. The key grammar points are highlighted in the exercises. It is designed

to assist teachers to organize in-class activities and consolidate the students' in-class acquisition.

We revised the textbooks based on the suggestions of textbook users. Outdated texts were changed, uncommonly used words were deleted, and new frequently used words were added. For the teachers' convenience, we replenished some exercises, and divided the original exercises into in-class exercises and homework. Thus, in-class exercises and homework have cooperation and division, mainly in-class exercises and homework as a supplement. Homework can be used as the flexible content for class teaching, some can be used for reviewing and examining on the second day.

Our guideline for this revision is to integrate phonetics, vocabulary, grammar and Chinese characters into the textbook and by the designed in-class activities, learners are able to transfer what is in the text into daily use and hence they can improve their language skills. To achieve this goal, we propose the following suggestions for teachers:

1. Pronunciation is a key and difficulty for language learners. Accordingly, we reserve the first ten lessons with the focus on pronunciation drills. Pronunciation drills are also distributed in each lesson. We hope that pronunciation drills can be varied according to students' pronunciation problems. Especially tones' practice, we intentionally extended the exercise of "Read aloud the syllables and pay attention to the tones" to the fourth volume. Most of Chinese words are disyllabic, mastering the tones of disyllabic words equates to mastering the tones of most of Chinese words. There are only 20 disyllabic tonal collocations, we selected the 20 syllables as the tone standard. When students make tonal mistakes, the tones of the 20 syllables can be used as a reference for them to correct. "Read aloud the syllables and pay attention to the tones" in lesson 1 to lesson 9 of the first volume is to read aloud the Pinyin, and from lesson 10 of the first volume on, this exercise is gradually transiting to read aloud Chinese characters.

2. Though the first volume focuses on pronunciation drills, Chinese characters

should also be involved in class. Teachers should help the students lay a good foundation of Chinese characters. "Table of Chinese characters' order of strokes" are attached in the first and second volumes. We deleted the column of "traditional Chinese characters" (traditional Chinese characters version can also be published if necessary), and reserved the columns of strokes, order of strokes and components of composite Chinese characters.

3. From the second volume to the eighth volume, the emphasis is on vocabulary. The glossary in each lesson includes new words in the text and exercises. According to "Beiyu mode", students are required to preview the new words before class, and have a basic command of "pronunciation" and "meaning" of the new words. The key of in-class practice is "pronunciation, meaning, use" of the words, especially the collocation and variation of the words. "Form" of the words can be practiced through homework.

4. Segregatory words are special language phenomena in Chinese, most of them are verbs. They are regarded as phrases in the first and second editions, and separately writing of Chinese Pinyin; some of them are regarded as words, parts of speech tagging as verbs, and continuously writing of Chinese Pinyin. In this version, segregatory words are regarded as words, parts of speech tagging as verbs, and continuously writing of Chinese Pinyin. Because its difficulty, teachers should pay attention to the practice of segregatory words for avoiding students' mistakes.

5. The course is compiled for foreign students, so some Pinyin of the new words are marked modified tones (including neutral tone), not the original tone in *Modern Chinese Dictionary (7th Edition)*. Thus, the students can smoothly learn and use Chinese language in daily life. Continuously writing of Chinese Pinyin of segregatory words is also base on the same principle.

6. Beijing pronunciation is the standard pronunciation of Putonghua, and the northern dialect is its basic dialect. According to this principle, we put "er" on the R-pronounced Words, for the students to learn authentic Chinese.

7. Teachers are expected to deal with the most frequently used grammatical rules

and explained them in as non-technical a way as possible. To achieve this, multi-media assistance, like pictures, body language and videos, can be used in class. In this way, students can be immersed in the language rather than lost in the grammatical jungle.

8. The texts are topic-centered and provide students with communication drills. The first volume to the fourth volume is mainly about campus life. From the fifth volume on, more social talks about Chinese culture, customs and ideas are involved. Teachers are expected to focus on the text and try to open students' mouths, improve their language ability and cultivate their language-learning potential.

9. "Functional conversations" is designed for this course every fifth or tenth lesson, with emphasis on "combining the linguistic structure with function". "Functional conversations" might be not closely related to the texts, but it is still a succinct summary.

10. Teachers can apply task-based approach in class and assign different communication tasks to students as much as possible. More in-class activities are strongly suggested. Hence, students are able to learn the language through communication and could be motivated by using the language.

Compilers

March, 2021

第1版前言

《速成汉语初级教程·综合课本》是为短期班零起点的外国学生编写的初级汉语教材（也可供长期班零起点的外国学生使用），教学时间为一个学期（20周），要求学生基本达到国内基础汉语教学一学年所达到的汉语水平。

速成教学时间短，要求高，只有实行“强化 + 科学化”的教学，才能成为最优化的教学。我们认为，速成教学的总体构想应该是：以掌握话题内容为教学的最低目的，以掌握话题模式为教学的最高目的，以掌握语法、功能为实现教学目的的具体措施和根本保障。因此，本教材的总体构想是：以话题为中心，以语法、功能为暗线，以全方位的练习为主体。

教材具体安排如下：共编80课，语音教学贯彻始终。1～10课突出语音（声母、韵母、声调），不涉及语法和功能；11～80课侧重于语法和功能，兼顾语音（难音、难调、重音、语调）。

编写课文时，我们慎重筛选和安排话题。有关生活、学习、交际方面的内容先出，介绍中国国情、中国人观念习俗的文化内容后出。其中，介绍中国国情的内容，以反映社会积极因素为主，但也有个别课文是反映社会消极因素的，避免脱离实际。课文内容的确定，均受一定语法点的制约，但又不捆得过死，注重语言的流畅性和趣味性。课文篇幅逐渐加长，但最长的不超过500字。

这套系列教材共出生词3400多个（专名未计算在内）。注音基本上以中国社会科学院语言研究所词典编辑室所编的《现代汉语词典》为依据，极个别的词参考了《汉语水平词汇与汉字等级大纲》。词性主要参考冯志纯等主编的《新编汉语多功能词典》。每课生词平均43个左右，只要求学生掌握本课重点词语。

语法点的选取主要依据国家对外汉语教学领导小组所编的《汉语水平等

级标准与语法等级大纲》。教材中涉及的语法点，甲级的除少数外全部出齐，乙级的出了大部分，丙级的也选取了一些。我们对少数语法点进行了调整，扩大了趋向补语、结果补语以及主谓谓语句的范围，增加了数量补语。语法难点分散出。对课文中出现的语法点，我们采取分别对待的处理方法：重点的语法点注释略多些，次重点的语法点注释从简，非重点的语法点不加注释，如连动句、兼语句等。语法点不是见一个注一个，基本上采取归纳法，并注意说明使用条件。

这套系列教材共选取100多个功能项目。这些功能项目都是学生最常见、最急用的。对这些功能项目也采取归纳法，而且是在逢五逢十的课中归纳。所归纳的功能项目只具有提示作用，在句型上不求全，教师上课时可根据教学实际情况适当补充。

我们所设计的练习是为教师备课、组织课堂教学、对学生进行技能训练服务的，说到底，是为提高学生的语言交际能力服务的。为此，我们采用了"语音→词语→句型→功能→成段表达→篇章结构→阅读理解"一条龙的练习模式。这些练习为帮助学生打好语音基础、实现从单句表达到成段表达的平稳过渡提供了可靠的保障。

我们的教材编写工作一直是在校领导和国家对外汉语教学领导小组办公室的大力支持下、在院领导的具体指导下、在学院同志的热情帮助下进行的。没有上上下下的通力合作，这套教材是编不出来的。

在教材编写过程中，我们召开过院内专家咨询会、校内专家咨询会，参加过合肥教材问题研讨会。与会专家对我们的教材初稿提出了许多宝贵意见，使我们的修改工作有了准绳。

在编写课文时，我们参考了校内外的有关教材，如韩鉴堂编的《中国文化》、赵洪琴等主编的《汉语写作》、刘德联等编的《趣味汉语》、吴晓露等主编的《说汉语谈文化》、潘兆明主编的《汉语中级听力教程》、吕文珍主编的《五彩的世界》等，从中受益匪浅。

在此，我们谨向有关领导、专家、同行和所有直接或间接帮助过我们的同志表示衷心的感谢。限于水平，教材的缺点和错误在所难免，恳请使用者给予批评指正。

编　者

1995年12月

Preface for the First Edition

Short Term Intensive Elementary Chinese is a Chinese language textbook designed for foreigners at elementary level in short term classes. It can, however, also be used for long term classes. The course covers one semester (20 weeks), students are expected to reach the basic level of one year regular Chinese language learning in China.

Intensive Chinese teaching requires "intensify + science". We think that the basic principle is: the minimum teaching aim is to master the topic contents, the maximum teaching aim is to master the topic mode, and the ultimate aim is to have a good command of grammar and function. In short, the overall design of the textbooks is centered on the topics, grammar and function as inherent clues, and accompanied with various exercises.

The textbooks consist of 80 texts and with pronunciation teaching throughout. Lesson 1 to Lesson 10 deals with pronunciation (initials, finals and tones), and without grammar and function involved. Lesson 11 to Lesson 80 focuses on grammar and function, with pronunciation involved (difficult syllables, tones, stress, and intonation).

Topics are carefully selected for compiling the texts. Topics from daily life are preferable, and then topics related to Chinese culture and customs. Positive aspects of Chinese society are highlighted, however, negative aspects are reserved for authenticity. The texts are restricted by grammar points in some extent, but language's fluency and interest are still pursued. The length of texts is added progressively, no more than 500 words.

The textbooks include over 3,400 words (excluding the proper nouns). Pronunciation is mostly based on *Modern Chinese Dictionary* compiled by dictionary department of Institute of Linguistics at Chinese Academy of Sciences. Some words are based on *Syllabus of Graded Words and Characters for Chinese Proficiency*. Parts of speech are mainly based on *The Newly Compiled Chinese Multiple Functional Dictionary* chiefly compiled by Feng Zhichun and so on. Each text consists of about 43 new words, students are required to have a good command of key words and phrases.

Grammar points are basically selected according to *Chinese Proficiency Graded Standard and Grammar Syllabus* compiled by China National Office for Teaching Chinese as a Foreign Language. Most of grammar points of class-A are included, as well as those of class-B. Grammar points of class-C are also selected. We have adjusted some of the grammar points, and extended the scope of directional complement, resultative complement and clausal predicate sentence, etc. Quantitive complement is also added. We have interpreted the grammar points in different ways: key grammar points are explained in detail, less important grammar points are explained in brief, and non-key grammar points are omitted, for example, sentences with serial verbs and pivotal sentences, etc. The inductive method has been adopted, with explanations to the condition of usage.

Over 100 functional items have been selected in the textbooks, which are useful and practical. These items have been summarized every fifth and tenth lesson. Sentence patterns might not be all covered, teachers can replenish it according to their teaching needs.

The exercises have been designed for teachers' lesson preparation and classroom organization, as well as for students' skills training. In the long run, the exercises aim to improve students' communication skills. We adopted the exercise mode: "pronunciation→words and phrases→sentence patterns→function→expressions in paragraph→discourse structure→reading comprehension". The exercises can be helpful to lay a solid foundation in students' pronunciation and communication skills.

The textbooks have been supported by our university and China National Office for Teaching Chinese as a Foreign Language, as well as our colleagues. Without them, the textbooks cannot be published.

While compiling the textbooks, seminars among experts of our university and college were held. We also attended the conference in Hefei on textbooks. Those experts have given us many helpful suggestions, which are very useful and constructive.

Many textbooks have been used as reference. These books are: *Chinese Culture* (compiled by Han Jiantang), *Chinese Writing* (chiefly compiled by Zhao Hongqin and so on), *Interesting Chinese* (compiled by Liu Delian and so on), *Talking about Chinese Culture* (chiefly compiled by Wu Xiaolu and so on), *Chinese Intermediate Listening Course* (chiefly compiled by Pan Zhaoming), *The Colorful World* (chiefly compiled by Lyu Wenzhen).

We would like to express our sincere thanks to those who have given us direct or indirect help. Because of our limited knowledge, mistakes are inevitable, your suggestions are very much appreciated.

Compilers

December, 1995

第2版前言

《速成汉语基础教程·综合课本》是《速成汉语初级教程·综合课本》的修订版。在修订过程中，我们保持原教材的优势和特色：

1. 全书共出词语3600多个，基本涵盖了《汉语水平词汇与汉字等级大纲》中的甲、乙两级词汇，另有一部分丙级词和超纲词。学完本教程的学生有望通过较高等级的HSK考试。

2. 原教材选取了贴近学生生活、学了就能用的话题，这样的内容学生喜欢学、愿意学。课文语言自然流畅、风趣幽默，能够引起学生的学习兴趣，激发他们的学习积极性。

3. 原教材语法点的讲解基本采用归纳法，课文编写不受语法点的绝对限制，允许冒出新的语法点。多年的教学经验证明，对成年人的汉语教学，首先要使他们对各种语言现象形成真切的感性认识，到一定阶段再进行归纳总结，帮助他们上升到理性认识，这样才符合第二语言教学的规律。

4. 原教材设计的练习大都紧紧围绕课文和当课的语法点，针对当课的重点和难点，能够很好地为教师备课、组织课堂教学、对学生进行语言技能和语言交际技能的训练服务。

原教材使用了10多年，我们也发现一些问题，如有的内容过时，有的练习显得臃肿，有的语法点解释过于烦琐等。这次修订，我们做的主要工作如下：

1. 为学生使用方便，把原教材的四册拆分为八册。本教程是为短期班零起点的外国学生编写的基础汉语教材，原教材80课共四册，每册20课，课本厚，内容多，学生短期内学不完，所以不适合短期班学生选择使用。修订后每册10课，便于教学单位根据学生实际水平灵活选用。学生能够在短期内学完一册课本，也会很有成就感和满足感。

2. 与时俱进，替换了部分课文。原教材中有些过时的内容都已撤换，另外增加了一些新鲜的词语，如“网吧”“上网”“手机”“短信”“数码相机”“MP3”“电子邮件”等等。

3. 压缩了部分练习。原教材的练习丰富有效，但是受教学时间限制，课上不能全部完成，短期班学生又不宜留过多的家庭作业，因此我们精简了练习项目，有些内容移到了与之配套的《速成汉语基础教程·听说课本》中。

4. 精简了语法点的注释。为贯彻“强化词语教学，淡化句法教学”的原则，并且考虑到短期班学生不一定要掌握系统的语法，我们把原教材中过于烦琐的语法注释删去，以便于教师讲解和学生记忆。

修订这套教材，我们总的指导思想是：以语音、词汇、语法、汉字等语言要素的教学为基础，通过课堂教学，帮助学生把语言要素转化为语言技能，进而转化为语言交际技能。为此，我们提出以下教学建议：

1. 由于语音是学生语言能力的门面，也是对外汉语教学的难点之一，我们保留了作为语音集中教学阶段的前10课，同时在各课中仍然进行分散的语音训练，希望教师根据学生的发音问题，有选择、有重点地加强语音训练。

2. 第一册的重点虽然是语音训练，但教师在突出听说训练的同时，也要重视汉字的认读和书写练习，帮助学生打好汉字基础。

3. 第二册到第八册的重点是词语教学。每课生词表里的生词包括课文中的生词和练习中的生词，两部分生词同等重要。在教学中，我们希望教师带领学生完成课后的所有练习，并且重视词语的搭配和活用，帮助学生掌握好词语的“音、形、义、用”。

4. 语法讲解不追求系统性，力求简单明了，从结构入手，重视语义和语用功能的说明。教师可通过图片、动作、视频等各种直观手段展示语法点，再进行机械练习，最后落实到活用上，使学生置身于语言交际的情境中，而不是语法术语和概念中。

5. 课文以话题为中心，为学生提供交际的模式。第一册到第四册的重点是有关学习、生活方面的交际，从第五册开始话题逐渐向社会交际过渡，增加介绍中国国情、中国人的观念习俗等文化方面的内容。教师要尽量引导学生以课文为范本，说他们自己想说的话，以此训练学生的思维能力，开发他们的语言潜能，提高交际能力。

6. 教师可采用任务教学法，给学生布置各种交际任务，多组织课堂活动，要求学生使用语言完成交际任务，在交际中学习语言，强化他们学习语言的成就感，激发他们的学习积极性。

《速成汉语基础教程·综合课本》(1—8)(第2版)的主编为郭志良和杨惠元。在本教程的修订过程中，张志忠修改了部分插图，赵娅修改了部分语法注释的英文翻译，罗斌翻译了前言。

编　者

2007年2月

Preface for the Second Edition

Speed-up Chinese: Integrated Textbook is the revised version of *Short Term Intensive Elementary Chinese,* with the following advantages and features reserved:

1. With a vocabulary over 3,600, the textbooks cover class-A and class-B words of *Syllabus of Graded Words and Characters for Chinese Proficiency*. Words of class-C and higher are included as well. After learning this course, students are expected to pass the advanced level of HSK.

2. The materials we used are student-centered. The unrevised version provided students with materials from daily life, which can be put into practice immediately after class. In this way, we believe students would be highly motivated in their language acquisition.

3. We apply inductive method to elaborate the grammar points. We have briefly dealt with the most frequently used grammatical rules and explained them in as non-technical a way as possible. New grammar points are not strictly confined to certain text since long-year teaching experience shows that for adult-learners, a general impression for the language will help them form a stronger foundation for their language learning.

4. The exercises are closely related to the text. The key grammar points are highlighted in the exercises. It is designed to assist teachers to organize in-class activities and consolidate the students' in-class acquisition.

The unrevised version has been in use for over ten years. Great changes have been taken place in the world and also in Chinese language. To make the textbook adapt to the changes, we revised the book. For this revision, our main focuses are:

1. For the learners' convenience, we divided the original four volumes into eight.

The revised version targets at short-term beginners. The unrevised version includes 80 lessons distributed in four volumes, with each having 20 lessons. While the revised version has 10 lessons for each volume, it can better suit the needs of short-term beginners.

2. We keep our pace with the times and update the materials. New words, such as Internet café, surf online, cell-phone, text messages are added into the revised version.

3. We removed some of the exercises. The exercises in the unrevised version are abundant. In considering the short learning span, we cut some exercises to suit the short-term learners' needs. A portion of the exercises is transferred to the *Speed-up Chinese: Listening and Speaking*.

4. We simplified the notes and explanations for grammar points. For beginners, emphasis should be put on vocabulary rather than the sentences. We removed some lengthy and complex notes and simplified the explanation to meet the requirements of learners.

Our guideline for the revision is to integrate phonetics, vocabulary, grammar and Chinese characters into the textbook and by the designed in-class activities, learners are able to transfer what is in the text into daily use and hence they can improve their language skills. To achieve this goal, we proposed the following suggestions for teachers:

1. Pronunciation is a key to language learners' learning and communication success outside the classroom. Accordingly, we reserved the first ten lessons with the focus on pronunciation drills. Pronunciation drills are also distributed in each lesson. We hope that teachers can pay continuous attention to students' pronunciation.

2. Though the first volume focuses on pronunciation drills, Chinese characters should also be involved in class. Teachers should help the students lay a good foundation of Chinese characters.

3. From the second volume to the eighth volume, the emphasis is on vocabulary. The glossary in each lesson includes new words in the text and exercises. Teachers are expected to guide students to finish the exercises. Meanwhile, the collocation and

variation of the words should also be emphasized.

4. Teachers are expected to deal with the most frequently used grammatical rules and explained them in as non-technical a way as possible. To achieve this, multi-media assistance, like pictures, body language and videos, can be used in class. In this way, students can be immersed in the language rather than lost in the grammatical jungle.

5. The texts are topic-centered and provided students with communication drills. Volume 1 to volume 5 is mainly about campus life. From volume 5 on, more social talks about Chinese culture, customs and ideas are involved. Teachers are expected to focus on the texts and try to open students' mouths, improve their language ability and cultivate their language-learning potential.

6. Teachers can apply task-based approach in class and assign different communication tasks to students. More in-class activities are strongly suggested. Hence, students are able to learn the language through communication and could be motivated by using the language.

Speed-up Chinese: Integrated Textbook (1—8) (Second Edition) is chiefly compiled by Guo Zhiliang and Yang Huiyuan. Zhang Zhizhong redrew some of the pictures, Zhao Ya revised the English grammar notes and Luo Bin translated the English preface.

Compilers

February, 2007

CONTENTS
目　录

Dì-yī kè 第一课 风味小吃

一 课文 Text

（晚上九点多，电影招待会结束了。王才和彼得走出影厅，忽然觉得有点儿饿，他们来到一家小吃店。）

王　才：今天我请你尝尝风味小吃。

彼　得：小吃？什么是小吃？

王　才：你看，这些都是小吃，你要点儿什么？

彼　得：我都没吃过，你吃什么我吃什么。

王　才：那好，你先找个地方坐下，我来买。

（过了一会儿，王才买来了好几种小吃，放在桌子上）

彼　得：你怎么买了这么多？吃得了吗？

王　才：不多，我们慢慢吃，每种都尝尝。

彼　得：这种圆的是什么？

王　才：炸糕。这种长的是油条。一种是甜的，一种是咸的。

彼　得：（尝了尝）果然很好吃。

王　才：这是馄饨。你要是觉得淡，可以放点儿酱油；要是喜欢吃酸的，可以放点儿醋。

彼　得：这馄饨跟饺子差不多。

王　才：不太一样。吃饺子没有汤，吃馄饨要连汤一块儿吃。

彼　得：小吃的种类真多啊！

王　才：可不是！一般的小吃店都卖几十种，长的、方的、圆的、扁的，干的、稀的，冷的、热的，你喜欢吃什么，可以任意选择。

彼　得：各地小吃味道是不是不太一样？

王　才：对。南甜，北咸，东辣，西酸，不同地区的人有不同的口味。

彼　得：中国人常说："玩儿在上海，吃在广州。"广州的小吃很有特色吧？

王　才：广州人喜欢喝早茶。早上，人们一边喝茶，一边吃各种各样的小点心。他们点心样样都做得非常精致，真是色、香、味、形俱佳。我吃好了，你怎么样？还想要点儿什么吗？

彼　得：我也吃饱了，什么也不要了。

王　才：吃得满意吗？

彼　得：满意，满意，吃得真满足。我来买单吧。

王　才：已经付了。上次是你付的，这次该我了。

二 生词 New words

1. 招待会	（名）	zhāodàihuì	reception
招待	（动）	zhāodài	to entertain, to serve
2. 炸糕	（名）	zhágāo	fried cake
炸	（动）	zhá	to fry in deep oil, to deep fry
3. 油条	（名）	yóutiáo	deep-fried twisted dough sticks
4. 咸	（形）	xián	salty, salted
5. 果然	（副）	guǒrán	really, as expected, as things turn out
6. 馄饨	（名）	húntun	wonton, dumpling soup
7. 淡	（形）	dàn	tasteless, weak, not salty
8. 酱油	（名）	jiàngyóu	soy sauce

9. 醋	（名）	cù	vinegar
10. 种类	（名）	zhǒnglèi	kind, type, variety
类	（名、量）	lèi	kind, type; a measure word for categories
11. 方	（形）	fāng	square
12. 扁	（形）	biǎn	flat
13. 干	（形）	gān	dry
14. 任意	（副）	rènyì	at will, wantonly, arbitrarily
15. 选择	（动）	xuǎnzé	to choose, to select
16. 不同	（形）	bùtóng	different, distinct
17. 地区	（名）	dìqū	area, district, region
18. 口味	（名）	kǒuwèi	the flavor or taste of food, a person's taste
19. 早茶	（名）	zǎochá	morning tea
20. 各种各样		gèzhǒng-gèyàng	various kinds
21. 精致	（形）	jīngzhì	fine, exquisite, delicate
22. 形	（名）	xíng	shape, form
形状	（名）	xíngzhuàng	shape, form, appearance
23. 俱	（副）	jù	all, completely, entirely
24. 佳	（形）	jiā	good, fine
25. 买单	（动）	mǎidān	to pay a (restaurant) bill

补充词汇　Supplementary words

1. 计划	（动、名）	jìhuà	to plan; plan
2. 包子	（名）	bāozi	steamed stuffed bun
3. 进修	（动）	jìnxiū	to engage in advanced studies
4. 相同	（形）	xiāngtóng	the same, identical
5. 行动	（动）	xíngdòng	to act, to take action
6. 安排	（动）	ānpái	to arrange
7. 排队	（动）	páiduì	to line up, to form a line
排	（动、名）	pái	to arrange, to put in order; line, row
8. 想法	（名）	xiǎngfa	idea, opinion

9. 粽子	（名）	zòngzi	a pyramid-shaped dumpling made of glutinous rice wrapped in bamboo or reed leaves
10. 根	（量）	gēn	a measure word for slender objects
11. 馅儿	（名）	xiànr	(of food) stuffing, filling
12. 嫁	（动）	jià	(of a woman) to marry
13. 消息	（名）	xiāoxi	news, information
14. 秘密	（名）	mìmì	secret
15. 份	（量）	fèn	set of
16. 快餐	（名）	kuàicān	fast food, quick meal
17. 区别	（名）	qūbié	distinction, difference
18. 题目	（名）	tímù	title, topic
19. AA 制	（名）	AA zhì	go Dutch, Dutch treat

二 课堂练习 Exercises

（一）语音

1. 辨音辨调

gùrán	固然	rényì	仁义	bùtóng	不同
guǒrán	果然	rènyì	任意	pǔtōng	普通
jīngzhì	精致	jīhuà	激化	bāozi	包子
jǐngzhì	景致	jìhuà	计划	bàozhǐ	报纸
jìnxiū	进修	xiāngtōng	相通	xíngdòng	行动
jīngxiū	精修	xiāngtóng	相同	xīn tòng	心痛

2. 四音节声调

任意选择	选择工作	积极安排	安排参观
正确选择	选择单位	重新安排	安排房间
认真选择	选择方向	统一安排	安排教室

随便选择	选择机会	顺利安排	安排宿舍
排队买饭	进修英语	情况相同	方法不同
排队买票	进修俄语	条件相同	想法不同
排队买菜	进修法语	环境相同	面积不同
排队买肉	进修汉语	年纪相同	内容不同

3. 重音

（1）谁都喜欢他。

我什么消息也没听到。

这个星期天，我哪儿也不去。

他怎么也听不懂。

你哪天来都行。

（2）谁愿意去谁去。

你想说什么就说什么。

你怎么说，我就怎么做。

你买多少，我卖多少。

哪里有困难，他就到哪里去。

（二）词语

从本课生词表中选择合适的词语填空

（1）今天早上我在小吃店吃了一个＿＿＿＿＿＿，两根＿＿＿＿和一碗＿＿＿＿。

（2）12月31日晚上，学校举行新年＿＿＿＿，邀请各国留学生参加。

（3）这件小礼物不太贵，可是做得非常＿＿＿＿。

（4）你喜欢吃猪肉＿＿＿＿的饺子还是羊肉＿＿＿＿的？

（5）＿＿＿＿跟饺子不一样。

（6）孙小英＿＿＿＿给了彼得的哥哥。

（7）我告诉你一个好＿＿＿＿，你这次考试成绩全班第一。

（8）这是一个________，她谁也不告诉。

（9）他买了一份________，吃完以后马上去教室了。

（10）这个地区的人喜欢吃________的，做什么菜都放很多盐或者酱油。

（11）这个商店卖的西服有很多________，你可以任意________。

（12）我________明年夏天再来这里进修。

（13）这两个句子有什么________？

（14）中国人常常用茶来________客人。

（15）四川________的菜很辣，你能吃吗？

（16）这两篇文章内容________，肯定是一个人写的。

（17）春天到了，公园里开满了________的鲜花。

（18）明天你有什么________吗？

（19）这个菜色、香、味、形________。

（20）端午节那天，方老师送给我们每人一个________。

（21）你的文章________是什么？

（22）他们听到这个消息马上________起来。

（23）请问，买去上海的火车票在哪儿________队？

（24）昨天看京剧我坐在第五________。

（25）请大家________队上车。

（三）句型

1. 替换

（1）你吃什么我吃什么。

看

要

买

喝

戴

听

做

学

（2）A：你去还是他去？

B：谁去都行。

你讲	他讲	谁讲
你介绍	我介绍	谁介绍
问小张	问小李	问谁
帮小丁	帮小王	帮谁
邀请老刘	邀请老周	邀请谁
去故宫	去长城	去哪儿
住二层	住三层	住哪儿
用钢笔	用圆珠笔	用什么
坐公共汽车	坐出租车	坐什么

（3）A：有什么事儿吗？

B：没有什么事儿。

安排

计划

打算

规定

决定

区别

想法

消息

结果

秘密

（4）A：谁想去呢？

B：没人想去。

想要

想换

想娶她

想嫁给他

想等他

能改变

能解决

能解释

能掌握

能保证

（5）点心样样都精致。

学生	个个	努力
老人	个个	健康
小伙子	个个	精神
姑娘	个个	美丽
衣服	件件	漂亮
钢笔	支支	好用
文章	篇篇	重要
比赛	场场	精彩

2. 用括号里的词语改写下列句子

（1）你喜欢的，我也喜欢。（什么）

（2）我要买跟你一样的词典。（什么）

（3）你买三本，我也买三本。（几）

（4）你换500美元，我也换500美元。（多少）

（5）我邀请的人跟你邀请的人相同。（谁）

（6）我邀请的人跟你邀请的人相同。（哪些）

（7）你去那儿，我也去那儿。（哪儿）

（8）你走着去，我也走着去。（怎么）

（9）你在教室复习，我也在教室复习。（哪儿）

（10）你在教室复习，我也在教室复习。（什么地方）

（11）每个人都帮助过我。（谁）

（12）每个地方我都想去。（哪儿）

（13）坐车去、骑车去、走着去都行。（怎么）

（14）明天去、后天去都可以。（哪天）

（15）这些小吃我都没吃过。（哪种）

（16）这些小吃我都没吃过。（什么）

（17）题目个个都很难写。（哪）

（四）成段表达

（1）介绍一两种你们国家的方便食品。

（2）介绍一次去小吃店吃饭的经历。

四 家庭作业 Homework

（一）词语

1. 用下列生词至少组成两个短语

（1）形状：________ ________　（2）计划：________ ________

（3）想法：________ ________　（4）消息：________ ________

（5）秘密：________ ________　（6）区别：________ ________

（7）任意：________ ________　（8）招待：________ ________

（9）安排：________ ________　（10）精致：________ ________

（11）行动：________ ________　（12）题目：________ ________

2. 用“果然”完成句子

（1）天气预报说今天上午有雨，10点钟__________________。

（2）别人说这里的冬天很冷，1月的最低气温是零下20℃，来到这里，__________________。

（3）我想妈妈这个星期一定会给我打电话，今天________________。

（4）以前我听说北京的颐和园非常漂亮，来到这里，____________。

（5）去年艾米离开北京时说："明年我一定再来中国。"今年夏天，________________________。

（二）阅读

自己的账自己付

看完展览已经快12点了，王欢和艾米来到一家小吃店。王欢要了两碗馄饨、两个炸糕、两根油条，还有二两包子，一共28块4。艾米从钱包里拿出14块2交给王欢，说："这是我的饭钱。"

这时候，王欢想起了三年前的一件事。

那时候，他在美国的一所大学进修英语。有一次，他们班的一个美国同学邀请他去公园玩儿。他们在湖边一边散步，一边聊天儿。到了吃晚饭的时候，那位同学说："王，咱们一起去吃晚饭吧？"王欢以为他要请客，就客气地说："好，谢谢你的邀请。"他们走进一家饭馆儿，每人要了一份快餐。吃完以后，那位美国同学只付了自己的账。这时候，王欢才知道，按照美国人的习惯，邀请你一起吃饭不是请客，自己的账要自己付，这是AA制。

今天，他又遇到了相同的情况。

1. 读后回答

（1）王欢为什么想起了三年前的那件事？

（2）王欢为什么以为那位美国同学要请客？

（3）为什么说王欢又遇到了相同的情况？

2. 朗读课文

五 语法 Grammar

（一）疑问代词的活用　Extended uses of interrogative pronouns

1. 疑问代词用于任指。主要用于陈述句，不要求回答。可与副词"都/也"

搭配使用。例如：

An interrogative pronoun can be used to refer to anyone, anything, any time or any place. In this case, it is used in a declarative sentence which does not expect a reply and may be used with the adverb “都” or “也”. For example:

（1）谁都帮助过我。

（2）这个星期天，我哪儿也不去。

也可与另一个同形的但表示特指的疑问代词搭配使用，还可与人称代词或指示代词搭配使用。例如：

An interrogative pronoun can also be used with another interrogative pronoun of the same form which refers to a definite person, object, time or place, or with a personal pronoun or a demonstrative pronoun. For example:

（3）谁了解情况，谁就介绍一下。

（4）谁了解情况，他就介绍一下。

（5）哪里有困难，他就到哪里去。

（6）哪里有困难，他就到那里去。

2. 疑问代词用于虚指。用于陈述句时，不要求回答。例如：

An interrogative pronoun can be used in an indefinite way. In this case, it is used in a declarative sentence where there is no need for any reply. For example:

（1）我想吃点儿什么了。

（2）他想去哪儿玩玩儿。

但跟疑问语气助词“吗/吧”搭配使用时，则要求回答。例如：

When an interrogative pronoun is used with the interrogative modal particle “吗” or “吧” in a sentence, a reply is needed. For example:

（3）你有什么事吗？

（4）他的词典给谁借走了吧？

（二）量词重叠　Classifier reduplication

在汉语里，大多数量词可以重叠。量词重叠表示周遍意义，强调具有共性的所有个体无一例外。可重叠的量词，例如：个、样、只、件、间、把、条、种、张、本、包、辆、封、篇、棵、颗、支、架、双、幅、声、句、层、首、片、批、套、场、回等。量词的重叠形式可做小主语、状语或定语，经常与“都”连用。例如：

In Chinese, most of the classifiers can be reduplicated. The reduplication of them indicates inclusiveness and stresses that there is no exception in any of the individuals that share the general character. The classifiers which can be reduplicated include “个、样、只、件、间、把、条、种、张、本、包、辆、封、篇、棵、颗、支、架、双、幅、声、句、层、首、片、批、套、场、回” and so on. A classifier that is reduplicated can function as a secondary subject, adverbial and attributive, and is usually used with “都”. For example:

（1）这些小吃样样都很好吃。

（2）比赛的时候，他回回跑第一。

（3）封封来信都充满了热情。

Dì-èr kè
第二课 坐出租车的故事

一 课文 Text

一天晚上，山本要参加日本大使馆在北京饭店举行的招待会。招待会七点开始，因为是下班高峰时间，他五点就出门了。在学校门口等了半个小时，还没叫到出租车，他急得心里直冒火。正在这时，一辆浅蓝色的出租车从远处开来，山本连忙招手。

车停了，山本走上前，正要伸手拉车门，旁边一个弱弱的女声说道："对不起，先生，这辆车是我约的。"

"你约的？"山本愣了，他看见一个打扮得很时髦的年轻姑娘也来到了车旁边。他不明白是什么情况，于是说："我有急事，要打车去北京饭店。"

姑娘掏出手机，和气地说："先生，您看，这辆车真的是我约的。"

司机师傅也微笑着说："先生，是这位女士先约好的。"

看见山本失望的样子，姑娘对司机师傅说："师傅，虽然我们谁也不认识谁，但是，如果顺路的话，就让他也一起走吧。"

师傅想了想，说："还算顺路吧，多少得绕几分钟。您要是不介意，那就请这位先生赶快上车吧。"

山本坐上车，系好安全带，很礼貌地对姑娘说："今天真是太谢谢你了！你可以跟我说说怎么在手机上约出租车吗？"

姑娘回答道："不用客气。在手机上约车很容易，您在手机上下载个App就行了，注册、使用都很简单。常用的约车平台有好几个，我用的是滴滴。"

车到北京饭店时，差一刻七点。山本掏出一百块钱递给司机，说了声谢谢后就急忙往饭店里跑。"先生，车钱怎么能都让您付呢！""先生，还没找您钱呢。"姑娘和司机几乎同时说道。山本猛然站住，回过头来说："你们热心帮我，当然应该我付钱。师傅，钱不用找了。"说完朝出租车深深地鞠了一躬。

二 生词 New words

1. 大使馆	（名）	dàshǐguǎn	embassy
大使	（名）	dàshǐ	ambassador
2. 高峰	（名）	gāofēng	peak, summit, climax
3. 直	（副）	zhí	continuously
4. 冒火	（动）	màohuǒ	to burn with anger, to get angry
5. 浅	（形）	qiǎn	(of color) light
6. 招手	（动）	zhāoshǒu	to wave, to beckon
7. 伸	（动）	shēn	to stretch, to extend
8. 女声	（名）	nǚshēng	female voice
9. 愣	（动）	lèng	to be absent-minded, to become speechless because of astonishment
10. 时髦	（形）	shímáo	fashionable, stylish
11. 掏	（动）	tāo	to fish out, to pull out, to draw out
12. 和气	（形）	héqi	gentle, kind, polite
13. 微笑	（动、名）	wēixiào	to smile; smile
14. 顺路	（形）	shùnlù	along the same route, convenient road
顺	（动）	shùn	to be in the same direction as, with
15. 介意	（动）	jièyì	to mind, to care about
16. 赶快	（副）	gǎnkuài	in a hurry, at once
17. 系	（动）	jì	to tie, to fasten
18. 安全带	（名）	ānquándài	seat belt, safety belt
19. 礼貌	（形、名）	lǐmào	polite; politeness

20. 下载	（动）	xiàzài	to download
21. 注册	（动）	zhùcè	to register
22. 平台	（名）	píngtái	platform, terrace
23. 猛然	（副）	měngrán	suddenly, abruptly
24. 朝	（介）	cháo	towards
25. 深	（形）	shēn	deep
26. 鞠躬	（动）	jūgōng	to bow

补充词汇　Supplementary words

1. 车窗	（名）	chēchuāng	car window
2. 联系	（动）	liánxì	to relate, to contact
3. 消失	（动）	xiāoshī	to disappear, to vanish
4. 粗重	（形）	cūzhòng	(of voice, etc.) loud and jarring, gruff, rough
粗	（形）	cū	thick, wide
5. 根本	（副）	gēnběn	at all, utterly, entirely (usually used in negation)
6. 显得	（动）	xiǎnde	to look, to seem, to appear
7. 佩服	（动）	pèifu	to admire
8. 同样	（形）	tóngyàng	same, equal, similar
9. 理	（动）	lǐ	to pay attention to, to take notice of
10. 平静	（形）	píngjìng	calm, quiet, tranquil
11. 印象	（名）	yìnxiàng	impression
12. 男声	（名）	nánshēng	male voice
13. 黑	（形）	hēi	black
14. 亲切	（形）	qīnqiè	kind, cordial, warm

专名　Proper nouns

1. 北京饭店	Běijīng Fàndiàn	Beijing Hotel
2. 滴滴	Dīdī	Didi
3. 朱佳	Zhū Jiā	name of a person, usually a female
4. 和平路	Hépíng Lù	Heping Road
5. 徐春兰	Xú Chūnlán	name of a person, usually a female

二 课堂练习 Exercises

（一）语音

1. 辨音辨调

zhāoshōu	招收	chēchuāng	车窗	wēixiǎo	微小
zhāoshǒu	招手	chīchuān	吃穿	wēixiào	微笑
lǐmào	礼貌	zū chē	租车	shēnqǐng	申请
lǐmiàn	里面	zhùcè	注册	shénqíng	神情
mángrán	茫然	dàshī	大师	liánxì	联系
měngrán	猛然	dàshǐ	大使	liànxí	练习
xiāoshī	消失	cūzhòng	粗重	jièyì	介意
xiǎoshí	小时	chūzhòng	出众	qièyì	惬意

2. 四音节声调

根本不在	显得自信	微笑服务	佩服小王
根本不爱	显得快乐	微笑谈话	佩服小杨
根本不去	显得漂亮	微笑招手	佩服小刘
根本不是	显得愉快	微笑握手	佩服小吴
多多联系	联系工作	同样时髦	说出地名
常常联系	联系单位	同样着急	答出地名
早早联系	联系学校	同样漂亮	写出地名
快快联系	联系食宿	同样热闹	猜出地名

3. 重音

（1）他疼得直叫。

他高兴得跳了起来。

他激动得说不出话来。

他忙得忘了吃午饭。

（2）急得他出了一头汗。

累得他走不动路了。

渴得他嗓子直冒烟。

饿得他眼睛冒金花。

（二）词语

从本课生词表中选择合适的词语填空

（1）这个湖，南边比较________，北边有的地方非常________。

（2）我不想买白色的，给我拿一件________颜色的试试。

（3）她从钱包里________出100元。

（4）我跟他说话，可是他不________我。

（5）淘宝、京东是中国人最常用的网上购物________。

（6）司机打开空调后，让我把________关上。

（7）车开之后请不要把头________出车外。

（8）我的心情像湖水一样________。

（9）我对这件事儿一点儿________也没有，都忘光了。

（10）开始上课的时候，你们给老师________吗？

（11）孩子上学前，父母要教会他们自己穿衣服、________鞋带。

（12）那个商店的售货员说话________，我喜欢去那儿买东西。

（13）那个孩子没有________，从来不跟别人打招呼。

（14）小王今天________很高兴，一定遇到了什么好事儿。

（15）那种动物从地球上永远地________了。

（16）小刘今天有约会，穿得非常________。

（17）我们大学毕业以后已经20年没有________了，我不知道他现在在哪儿。

（18）我们国家的________举行招待会，邀请孙校长参加。

（19）你________走！他们在外边等你呢。

（20）公园里开满了各种颜色的花儿，有红的、黄的、紫的、________蓝的，好看极了。

（21）突然，一个粗重的________叫了起来："小心汽车！"

（22）一个黑头发（tóufa，hair）大眼睛的姑娘________着说："见到您很高兴。"

（三）句型

替换

（1）我们谁也不认识谁。

理

佩服

了解

喜欢

照顾

关心

怀疑

笑话

责怪

（2）他急得心里直冒火。

累	站不起来了
累	走不动了
忙	一点儿空儿也没有
忙	抽不出时间来
忙	三天没回家了

忙	连饭也没吃
气	一句话也说不出来
困	吃着饭就睡着了
高兴	跳了起来
高兴	跟孩子一样

（3）是<u>这位女士先约好</u>的。

我通知他开会

我把窗户打开

我把她送到医院

我先发现他

我最后一个离开这里

他先打了我

他第一个进门

他先提出这个问题

他先跟我打招呼

他把你的车弄坏

（四）成段表达

（1）讲述一次你坐出租车的经历。

（2）讲述一次你下载使用某个App的经历。

四 家庭作业 Homework

（一）词语

1. 用下列生词至少组成两个短语

（1）招手：________ ________　　（2）和气：________ ________

（3）礼貌：________ ________　　（4）微笑：________ ________

（5）猛然：________ ________　　（6）佩服：________ ________

（7）印象：________ ________　　（8）平静：________ ________

2. 用括号里的词语完成句子，注意使用补语

（1）听到这个好消息，他__________________。（激动）

（2）得到那么多人的帮助，他__________________。（感动）

（3）听说这次考试成绩不好，她__________________。（难过）

（4）小王得了气管炎，夜里__________________。（咳嗽）

（5）公共汽车上__________________。（挤）

（6）那个小伙子__________________。（强壮）

（7）那个孩子__________________。（笨）

（8）他两天没吃饭，__________________。（饿）

（9）这个地区变化真大，__________________。（变）

（10）考试的时候，她__________________。（紧张）

（二）阅读

朱佳送我回学校

我常坐出租车，遇见过各种各样的司机。有一位叫朱佳的姑娘给我留下了很深的印象。

那是去年冬天的一个晚上，已经快11点了，天下着大雪。因为手机没电了，身上也只有几块钱，我只好坐公共汽车回学校。在车站等了半天，也没见一个人，我很着急。正在这时，一辆出租车停在我身边。一个姑娘从车窗里伸出头来，亲切地说："小姐，末班车10点50就开走了，坐我的车吧。"我摇了摇头。她大概看出了我的难处，客气地问："你是农业大学的学生吧？"我看了看身上穿的校服外套，点了点头。"我家住在农大附近，正好顺路，免费送你回去。"说着，她把车门打开，让我上车。

她一边开车，一边跟我聊天儿。从谈话中，我知道她叫朱佳，今年

23岁，高中毕业没考上大学，当了出租车司机。她非常热爱自己的工作，为了更好地为乘客服务，她正在自学英语。她无意中说出她家住在和平路，根本不在农业大学附近。

朱佳把我送到学校门口，我说："我是澳大利亚留学生，中文名字叫徐春兰，我们可以加一下微信，以后你学习英语有什么困难都可以来找我，我可以帮助你。"她微笑着说："一回生两回熟，三回就是好朋友。以后我们常来常往，多多联系。"她关上车门，对我说了声"再见"就开车走了。我站在雪地里，看着她的车慢慢地消失在冬夜里，心情久久不能平静。

1. 不查词典，根据上下文猜猜下列词语的意思

(1) 末班车——

(2) 摇头——

(3) 难处——

(4) 免费——

(5) 乘客——

(6) 自学——

(7) 无意——

(8) 常来常往——

(9) 冬夜——

2. 读后回答

(1) 开始时徐春兰为什么不想坐出租车回学校?

(2) 徐春兰在车站等了半天，为什么周围没有人?

(3) "她大概看出了我的难处。"徐春兰的"难处"是什么?

(4) 徐春兰知道了朱佳的哪些情况?

(5) 徐春兰为什么要加朱佳的微信?

五 语法 Grammar

（一）状态补语（2） State complement (2)

有一种状态补语，位于结构助词“得”后边，既可用来描写动作结果的状态，也可用来描写主语的状态。这种状态补语可由形容词或形容词性短语充当，也可由动词性短语或主谓短语充当。而述语既可由动词充当，也可由形容词充当。例如：

There is a kind of state complement which is placed after the structural particle “得”. It is used to describe the state of the result of an action, or the state of the subject of an action. Adjectives, adjectival phrases, verbal phrases as well as subject-predicate phrases can act as this type of state complement. Both verbs and adjectives can be used as the predicates in such sentences. For example:

（1）他急得心里直冒火。

（2）他跑得跟兔子一样快。

（3）他累得站不起来了。

（4）他忙得一点儿空儿也没有。

（二）主谓谓语句（4） Clausal predicate sentence (4)

在汉语里有一种主谓谓语句，其大主语和小主语之间具有整体和部分的关系。例如：

In Chinese, there is a kind of clausal predicate sentence, in which there is a whole-part relationship between the subject and secondary subject. For example:

（1）我们俩你不认识我，我不认识你。

（2）我们谁也不认识谁。

（3）你说的话哪儿也对不上哪儿。

Dì-sān kè
第三课

我究竟算哪儿的人呢

一 课文 Text

（王才、丁兰、彼得和艾米在校园里聊天儿）

彼　得：丁兰，你家在北京吗？

丁　兰：我不是北京人，我家离这儿远着呢。

艾　米：丁小姐中等的个儿，苗条的身材，白白的皮肤，一看就知道是南方姑娘。

王　才：没错，她家在一个著名的旅游区。那儿青山绿水，风景可漂亮了。

丁　兰：钱塘江水从我家门前流过。站在阳台上，就能看见美丽的西湖。

艾　米：我知道了，是杭州。

丁　兰：你说对了。杭州是中国的六大古都之一，可美了。

彼　得：当然啦，那儿山美水美，人也美，不去太遗憾了！

艾　米：王才，你家在哪儿？

王　才：你猜猜。

艾　米：你个子不是很高，长得挺秀气，大概也是南方人吧？

王　才：不对，我是北方人。我的家乡有中外闻名的秦兵马俑，有历史悠久的大雁塔……好些朝代的首都都在西安，西安是中国的六大古都之首。

艾　米：你是西安人？

王　才：是，你去过西安吗？

艾　米：还没去过。下个月我准备去好好儿逛逛这座历史名城。

丁　兰：彼得，你是美国什么地方的人？

彼　得：这个问题对我来说太难回答了。

王　才：为什么？

彼　得：我是在旧金山出生的，出生后三个月就随父母迁居国外了。三年后，我们又搬回旧金山，接着在费城住了五年，在纽约生活了一年。后来，因为纽约物价上涨，生活费用太高，我爸爸一时失业，一家人又来到加利福尼亚，在一个小镇上租了一套房子……你说，我究竟算哪儿的人呢？

二 生词 New words

1. 究竟	（副）	jiūjìng	actually, exactly, after all
2. 着呢	（助）	zhene	(as an intensive at the end of a sentence, after adjectives or verbs that admit of differences of degree) very, quite
3. 个儿	（名）	gèr	height, stature, size
4. 苗条	（形）	miáotiao	slim, slender
5. 身材	（名）	shēncái	figure, stature
6. 皮肤	（名）	pífū	skin
皮	（名）	pí	skin, fur
7. 著名	（形）	zhùmíng	famous, well-known
8. 风景	（名）	fēngjǐng	scenery, landscape
9. 江	（名）	jiāng	(large) river
10. 流	（动）	liú	to flow
11. 阳台	（名）	yángtái	balcony

12. 古都	（名）	gǔdū	old or ancient capital
13. 秀气	（形）	xiùqi	delicate, elegant
14. 家乡	（名）	jiāxiāng	hometown
15. 塔	（名）	tǎ	tower, pagoda
16. 朝代	（名）	cháodài	dynasty
朝		cháo	dynasty, an emperor's reign, court
17. 首都	（名）	shǒudū	capital, metropolitan
首		shǒu	first
都		dū	capital, big city
18. 对……来说		duì…lái shuō	to sb./sth., for sb./sth.
19. 随	（动）	suí	to follow
20. 迁居	（动）	qiānjū	to move (house), to change residence
21. 国外	（名）	guówài	abroad, overseas, external
22. 物价	（名）	wùjià	commodity price
23. 上涨	（动）	shàngzhǎng	to rise, to go up
涨	（动）	zhǎng	to rise, to go up
24. 费用	（名）	fèiyong	cost, expenses
25. 失业	（动）	shīyè	to lose one's job, to be out of work
26. 镇	（名）	zhèn	town
27. 租	（动）	zū	to rent

补充词汇　Supplementary words

1. 回忆	（动）	huíyì	to recall, to call to mind
2. 分配	（动）	fēnpèi	to distribute, to assign, to allot
3. 清	（形）	qīng	clear, unmixed
4. 头发	（名）	tóufa	hair
5. 无论如何		wúlùn-rúhé	in any case, whatever happens
6. 指	（动）	zhǐ	to point at, to point to, to refer to
7. 不仅	（连）	bùjǐn	not only
仅	（副）	jǐn	only, merely
8. 不是…… 而是……		bú shì… ér shì…	not...but...
9. 嘴唇	（名）	zuǐchún	lip

10. 弯	（形）	wān	curved, bent
11. 眉毛	（名）	méimao	eyebrow, brow
12. 洁白	（形）	jiébái	pure white, spotlessly white
13. 牙齿	（名）	yáchǐ	tooth
14. 采	（动）	cǎi	to pick, to gather
15. 拣	（动）	jiǎn	to pick up, to pick out, to choose

专名 Proper nouns

1. 钱塘江	Qiántáng Jiāng	the Qiantang River
2. 大雁塔	Dàyàn Tǎ	the Great Wild Goose Pagoda
3. 旧金山	Jiùjīnshān	San Francisco
4. 费城	Fèichéng	Philadelphia
5. 纽约	Niǔyuē	New York
6. 加利福尼亚	Jiālìfúníyà	California
7. 北京外国语大学	Běijīng Wàiguóyǔ Dàxué	Beijing Foreign Studies University

三 课堂练习 Exercises

（一）语音

1. 辨音辨调

shēncái	身材	chūmíng	出名	fēngjǐng	风景
shēngcái	生财	zhùmíng	著名	fēngjìng	风镜
yántán	言谈	wújià	无价	shīyè	失业
yángtái	阳台	wùjià	物价	shíyè	实业
huíyì	回忆	búlùn	不论	shàngzhǎng	上涨
huìyì	会议	wúlùn	无论	shàngchǎng	上场

2. 四音节声调

首都机场	分配工作	生活费用	南方姑娘
首都剧场	分配宿舍	招待费用	北方姑娘
首都医院	分配时间	学习费用	城市姑娘
首都影院	分配房子	办公费用	农村姑娘
历史悠久	山美水美	长得精神	好吃着呢
历史时期	山清水秀	长得苗条	好听着呢
历史原因	青山绿水	长得好看	好玩着呢
历史名城	千山万水	长得秀气	好看着呢

3. 语调

（1）不去太遗憾了！

不看太遗憾了！

不逛太遗憾了！

不住太遗憾了！

（2）这个问题对我来说太难回答了。

这个问题对我来说太难解决了。

这个问题对我来说太难解释了。

这个问题对我来说太难理解了。

（二）词语

从本课生词表中选择合适的词语填空

（1）北京是中国的________。

（2）这里的________真美。

（3）我们学校有很多________的教授。

（4）这条小河从山上________下来，河水真________。

（5）贝拉白________，蓝眼睛，黄________，一看就知道是欧洲姑娘。

（6）明天我________________都要去医院看看张老师。

(7) 小孙昨天刚从________回来，今天就开始工作了。

(8) 这件事使我________起小时候的一件事。

(9) 这个城市有很多工人________了，他们的生活很困难。

(10) 站在我家的________上可以看见西山。

(11) 他说的家乡是________老家，不是这里的家。

(12) 他用手________了一下自己，又________了一下外边，意思是他想去外边。

(13) 你昨天说去，今天又说不去，你________去不去？

(14) 学校外边有一个书店可以________书，一本书一天一块钱。

(15) 他们全家从一个大城市________到这个小________来了。

(16) 这个商店________服务态度好，而且________便宜。

(17) 他________不会，________粗心，所以这道题又做错了。

(18) 不是因为她的________不苗条，而是因为衣服大小不合适。

(19) 这个建筑是哪个________修建的，谁也不知道。

(20) 我身上________有10块钱了。

（三）句型

1. 替换

(1) 丁小姐中等的个儿，苗条的身材。

苗条的身材	白白的皮肤
白白的皮肤	高高的个子
高高的个子	大大的眼睛
大大的眼睛	秀气的鼻子
秀气的鼻子	红红的嘴唇
大大的眼睛	弯弯的眉毛
黑黑的头发	白白的皮肤
红红的嘴唇	洁白的牙齿

（2）我家离这儿远着呢。

那个工厂	大
那座山	高
那条路	长
那条河	宽
那儿的物价	高
那个地方	好玩儿
那个电影	好看
那件事	麻烦
那个老师	年轻
那个姑娘的身材	苗条

2. 用“着呢”改写句子

（1）那个地方特别冷，别去了。

（2）外边真凉快，快出来吧。

（3）屋子里真暖和，快进来吧。

（4）那个公园很大，一天也逛不完。

（5）谁说那个地方人少，那个地方人非常多。

（6）过春节的时候特别热闹。

（7）我渴极了，给我点儿水吧。

（8）这中药怎么这么苦，我不想吃了。

（9）这个西瓜真甜，快尝尝。

（10）那个商店的售货员特别热情，我喜欢去那儿买东西。

（四）成段表达

（1）描述图片中的这个人

（2）描述图片中的这个地方

四 家庭作业 Homework

（一）词语

用下列生词至少组成两个短语

（1）著名：________ ________　　（2）风景：________ ________

（3）迁居：________ ________　　（4）物价：________ ________

（5）失业：________ ________　　（6）回忆：________ ________

（7）采：________ ________　　（8）拣：________ ________

（二）阅读

我的家乡在山区

我是个老北京了。我是1960年考上北京外国语学院的，就是现在的北京外国语大学，1964年毕业后分配到这里工作。在北京已经生活60多年了，可我还是常常想家。你别误会，我说的“家”，当然不是指北京的这个家，而是指我的老家。

我的老家在山区。那里清清的河水，高高的山，一片一片的果树林，一层一层的梯田（tītián，terraced fields）。我多想回去看看家乡的山山水水呀！

我爱我的家乡，不仅是因为家乡的美丽，还因为那里有我的亲人，有我的童年（tóngnián，childhood）。记得小时候常跟伙伴们一起玩儿，春天去山上采野花儿，夏天到河里去摸鱼，秋天拣栗子（lìzi，chestnut），冬天打秋千（dǎ qiūqiān，to have a swing）。我多想回去看看小时候的朋友们哪！

是啊，回一趟老家可真不容易！以前得先坐七八个小时的火车，再换汽车，下了汽车，还得走几十里的山路，麻烦着呢。现在高铁通了，回一趟老家方便不少。我决定，无论如何，每年我都要回一趟老家。

1. 解释词语

（1）老北京——

（2）老家——

（3）童年——

（4）小时候——

（5）伙伴——

（6）山路——

2. 根据课文内容填空

（1）“我”在北京已经生活________年了。

（2）“我”常想自己的________。

(3)“我”的家乡在________。那里________________，________，一片一片的________，一层一层________。风景________！

(4)“我”和小伙伴们春天______________，夏天____________，秋天________________，冬天________________，玩儿得可有意思了。

(5)以前，“我”回一趟老家很不________，得先坐________，再换________，下了汽车，还得走________________。

(6)现在__________，回一趟老家______________。“我”决定，无论如何，每年“我”都要________________。

3. 朗读课文

（三）写作

以前你生活在A城市，现在你来到B城市。写一篇文章介绍城市A和城市B的相同和不同之处，以及你本人的改变。

五 语法 Grammar

（一）名词谓语句（2） Nominal predicate sentence (2)

汉语描写主语所代表的人、事物或处所的状态时，谓语可由名词或名词性短语充当。名词性短语中的定语多是形容词、数量词。例如：

In Chinese, nouns or nominal phrases can be used as predicates to describe the status of people, things or places that function as the subjects. The attributives in the nominal phrases are often adjectives and numeral classifier phrases. For example:

（1）丁小姐中等的个儿，苗条的身材，白白的皮肤。

（2）那儿青山绿水，风景可漂亮了。

（3）桌子前边两把椅子、一个茶几。

（二）动态助词“着呢” The aspectual particle “着呢”

动态助词“着呢”用于形容词或形容词性短语之后，表示程度高，略带夸张意味。例如：

The aspectual particle “着呢” is used after adjectives or adjectival phrases to indicate a high degree with a tone of exaggeration. For example:

（1）我家离这儿远着呢。

（2）那条山路难走着呢。

注意：（1）限于口语。（2）形容词或形容词性短语前边不能加程度副词，后边也不能带程度补语。

Points for attention: (1) The aspectual particle “着呢” is only used in spoken language. (2) Adjectives or adjectival phrases may neither be preceded by degree adverbs nor followed by degree complements.

六 注释 Notes

六大古都 The six ancient capitals of China

中国的六大古都指北京、西安、开封、洛阳、南京和杭州。

The six ancient capitals of China refer to Beijing, Xi’an, Kaifeng, Luoyang, Nanjing and Hangzhou.

Dì-sì kè 第四课 友谊是无价的

一 课文 Text

最近，王才又交了一个新朋友。他是英国人，名叫吉姆。

说起来很有意思。王才和吉姆成为朋友，是和吉姆的两次感谢分不开的。

第一次是上星期六下午。那天，大风把宿舍楼下的自行车全都刮倒了，王才要骑车去买东西，他扶起自己的车，顺便又把旁边的车一辆一辆地扶了起来。这一切正巧让出门骑车的吉姆看到了，他跑上前，紧紧地握住王才的手，连声表示感谢。

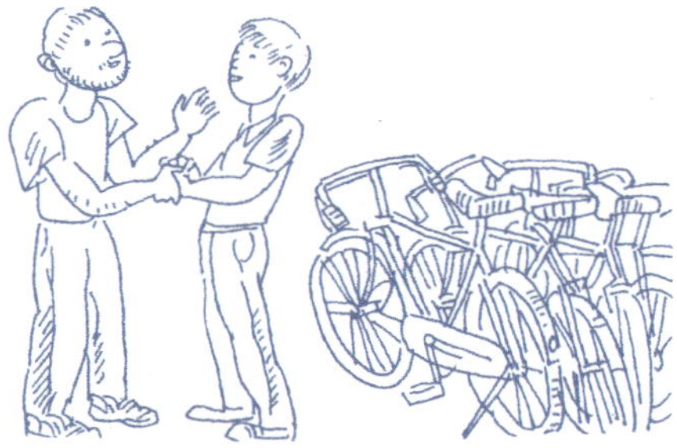

"不用谢！"王才笑着说。

"当然要谢。"

"就因为扶起了几辆自行车吗？这点儿小事儿谁都能做。"

"你只说对了一半儿。"吉姆认真地说，"当然，谁也不认为这是件大事儿。这种小事儿人人都做得了，可不是所有的人都愿意去做。你说是不是？"

接着，两个人分别做了自我介绍，他们互相认识了。

第二次是前几天，王才在一场足球比赛中受了伤，脚疼得很厉害。当天晚上10点多钟，吉姆来了。他说："对不起，这么晚了还来打搅你。我刚从外面回来，听说你受了伤，来看看你。这是一盒儿英国产的止痛膏，效果不错，你贴上试试。”说着，他帮王才脱下袜子，亲手把药膏贴在他的脚上，并且嘱咐王才：“明天哪儿也别去，在宿舍好好休息。”

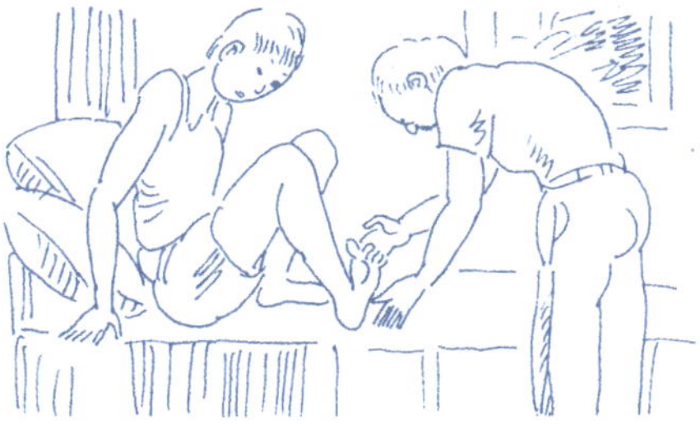

王才感动得不知说什么好，他只说了一声：“谢谢你，吉姆！”

“其实，说谢谢的应该是我。”

“为什么？”

“因为你是第一个不问价钱就接受我帮助的人。如果你问我这药多少钱，那就说明你还没把我当成朋友。谢谢你把我当成了朋友。”吉姆说完就高兴地告辞了。

“是啊，吉姆说得很对。”王才心想，“药是有价的，而真正的友谊是无价的。”

二 生词 New words

1. 无价	（动）	wújià	to be beyond price
无	（动）	wú	to not have, there is not
2. 分不开		fēn bu kāi	to be inseparable, to be combined with
分开	（动）	fēnkāi	to separate, to divide
分	（动）	fēn	to divide, to part
3. 扶	（动）	fú	to straighten sth. up, to support with the hand
4. 正巧	（副）	zhèngqiǎo	just in time, just at the right time, as it happens
5. 连声	（副）	liánshēng	(to say) again and again, repeatedly
6. 自我	（代）	zìwǒ	self, oneself
7. 脚	（名）	jiǎo	foot
8. 当天	（名）	dàngtiān	the same day, that very day

9. 打搅	（动）	dǎjiǎo	to disturb, to trouble
10. 产	（动）	chǎn	to produce, to yield
11. 止痛膏	（名）	zhǐtònggāo	analgesic patcher or ointment
痛	（形）	tòng	painful, sore
12. 效果	（名）	xiàoguǒ	effect, result
13. 脱	（动）	tuō	to take off, to strip
14. 亲手	（副）	qīnshǒu	with one's own hands, personally
15. 药膏	（名）	yàogāo	ointment, salve
16. 嘱咐	（动）	zhǔfu	to tell, to exhort
17. 价钱	（名）	jiàqian	price
18. 说明	（动）	shuōmíng	to prove, to restify, to explain
19. 告辞	（动）	gàocí	to take leave, to say goodbye to

补充词汇　Supplementary words

1. 脾气	（名）	píqi	temper
2. 打扰	（动）	dǎrǎo	to disturb, to trouble
3. 复活	（动）	fùhuó	to bring back to life, to revive
复		fù	again, repeatedly
4. 深情	（形、名）	shēnqíng	soulful; deep feeling, deep love
5. 衷心	（形）	zhōngxīn	heartfelt, cordial, wholehearted
6. 医生	（名）	yīshēng	doctor
7. 召开	（动）	zhàokāi	to convene
8. 教育	（动、名）	jiàoyù	to educate, to inculcate; education
9. 绣	（动）	xiù	to embroider
10. 朵	（量）	duǒ	a measure word for flowers
11. 海员	（名）	hǎiyuán	sailor, seaman
12. 辛苦	（形）	xīnkǔ	hard, toilsome, laborious
13. 勿	（副）	wù	do not
14. 户	（量）	hù	a measure word for families
15. 轧	（动）	yà	to run over, to roll
16. 劳动	（动、名）	láodòng	to labor, to work; work, labor
17. 彩色	（名）	cǎisè	color, colorful
18. 经验	（名）	jīngyàn	experience
19. 乡	（名）	xiāng	country, village, township

20. 讨厌	（动）	tǎoyàn	to dislike, to be disgusted with
21. 任何	（代）	rènhé	any, whichever, whatever
22. 害怕	（动）	hàipà	to be afraid, to be scared
23. 手指	（名）	shǒuzhǐ	finger

专名 Proper nouns

1. 英国	Yīngguó	Britain, the United Kingdom
2. 吉姆	Jímǔ	Jim

二 课堂练习 Exercises

（一）语音

1. 辨音辨调

zhēn qiǎo	真巧	liánshēng	连声	dǎjiǎo	打搅
zhèngqiǎo	正巧	luánshēng	孪生	dà jiǎo	大脚
xiǎo huǒ	小火	zhǔfu	嘱咐	píqi	脾气
xiàoguǒ	效果	zhùfú	祝福	bíqi	荸荠
dǎrǎo	打扰	fùhé	复合	shēnqíng	深情
dǎsǎo	打扫	fùhuó	复活	shēngqín	生擒
zhōngxīn	衷心	fēnkāi	分开	qīnshǒu	亲手
zhuānxīn	专心	fènkǎi	愤慨	qínshòu	禽兽

2. 四音节声调

中国医生	嘱咐小王	当天上午	效果很好
韩国医生	嘱咐小杨	当天中午	效果挺好
美国医生	嘱咐小常	当天下午	效果不错
外国医生	嘱咐小黄	当天晚上	效果不好

骑车上班	自我介绍	认真地说	召开大会
骑车上街	自我教育	认真地读	召开茶会
骑车进城	自我批评	认真地写	召开酒会
骑车回家	自我表扬	认真地看	召开班会

3. 重音

（1）这点儿小事儿谁都能做。

这点儿小事儿谁都能干。

这点儿小事儿谁都能办。

这点儿小事儿谁都能解决。

（2）药是有价的，而真正的友谊是无价的。

画儿是有价的，而真正的友谊是无价的。

黄金是有价的，而真正的友谊是无价的。

花儿是有价的，而真正的友谊是无价的。

（二）词语

从本课生词表中选择合适的词语填空

（1）小黄经常照顾这个________儿________女的老人。

（2）对你们的帮助我表示________的感谢。

（3）你吃不了一个面包，________给我一半儿吧。

（4）那个姑娘在衣服上________了一朵花。

（5）________们在船上工作，他们非常________。

（6）你看，门上挂着"请勿______________"的牌子，彼得可能睡觉了。

（7）这几天他总是________________我，真受不了。

（8）我父亲的________不好，他常常跟母亲发________。

（9）这个小镇上每家每________都买了小汽车。

（10）你怎么不问问________就买？你又上当了。

（11）今天我在路上看见一辆汽车________伤了一个小孩儿。

(12) 下个月有个重要的国际会议在我们大学________。

(13) 我从小时候就喜欢________，常常帮助父母干活儿。

(14) 感觉这张________照片没有那张黑白的效果好。

(15) 我刚要给王才打电话，________他来了。

(16) 这种药治感冒________不错，我吃了三片儿就好了。

(17) 我们班的老师都很有________，教学________非常好。

(18) 我的________在踢球的时候受了伤。

(19) 你要是热就把衣服________了吧。

(20) 你的这种态度________你不喜欢他。

(21) 教师是做________工作的人。

(22) 我们________就知道了考试成绩。

(三) 句型

替换

(1) 谁都认为这是件大事儿。

这是件好事儿

他是好人

他是老实人

他是聪明人

那儿很安静

那本词典很有用

这儿条件很好

这些产品质量不错

(2) 谁也不认为这是件大事儿。

这是件好事儿

他是坏人

他应该去

他说得对

他有道理

他没有经验

教育不重要

教师不辛苦

（3）明天你哪儿也别去。

明天	我	哪儿	不去
昨天	我	哪儿	没去
明天	你	什么	别做
明天	我	什么	不做
昨天	我	什么	没做
这事儿	你	谁	别告诉
这事儿	我	谁	不告诉
这事儿	我	谁	没告诉

（4）人人都做得了。

家家	吃饺子
户户	有了汽车
村村	修了公路（gōnglù，highway）
乡乡	通了公共汽车
他事事	不顺利
他月月	有进步
他年年	有新的变化

（四）成段表达

（1）讲一件助人为乐的事情

（2）你认为友谊是无价的吗？

四 家庭作业 Homework

（一）词语

1. 用下列生词至少组成两个短语

（1）连声：________ ________　　（2）亲手：________ ________

（3）正巧：________ ________　　（4）教育：________ ________

（5）嘱咐：________ ________　　（6）说明：________ ________

（7）辛苦：________ ________　　（8）衷心：________ ________

（9）经验：________ ________　　（10）效果：________ ________

（11）讨厌：________ ________　　（12）脾气：________ ________

2. 用括号里的词语改写句子

（1）人人都喜欢他的表演。（谁）

（2）任何人都不喜欢战争。（谁）

（3）没有人愿意参加她的生日晚会。（谁）

（4）每个人都讨厌他。（谁）

（5）明天你任何地方也不能去。（哪儿）

（6）这种丝绸任何商店也买不到。（哪儿）

（7）你任何时候来我都欢迎。（什么）

（8）你不要买任何东西。（什么）

（9）他任何会议都不参加。（什么）

（10）他任何事情都不害怕。（什么）

（二）阅读

断指“复活”

乔治是个外国海员，30多岁，高高的个子。他常到中国来，能说一口流利的汉语。前年夏天，他们的船来到上海。工作的时候，乔治的四根手指被机器轧断了，大家赶紧把他送到附近的医院。

在医院里，乔治着急地对中国医生说："大夫，这是一只劳动的手啊！没有它，我们全家怎么活呀？"医生们安慰他："你放心吧，我们一定把你的手指接上。"手术做得非常成功，乔治的手指接上以后很快"复活"了，吃饭、写字都没有问题。出院不久，他就回国了。

今年春天，乔治又来到中国。他去医院看望给他做手术的大夫，并且送给他们一件礼物。医生们打开包装一看，原来是一块儿丝绸，上面用彩色的线绣着"友谊"两个大字。乔治深情地说："我的这只手是你们给的。我用你们给的这只手绣了这两个字，表示对你们的衷心感谢！"

医生们拿着这件珍贵的礼物，心情特别激动。他们珍惜这件礼物，更珍惜乔治对中国人民的友谊。

1. 看第一遍后选择正确答案

（1）乔治的手指是怎么断的？

A. 被机器轧断的

B. 自己弄断的

（2）"没有它，我们全家怎么活呀？"是什么意思？

A. 没有它，我们全家用什么生活

B. 没有它，我们全家不能生活

（3）乔治说："我的这只手是你们给的。"意思是：

A. 中国医生给了他一只手

B. 中国医生治好了他的手

（4）乔治为什么亲手绣了"友谊"两个字送给中国大夫？

A. 表示对中国医生的衷心感谢

B. 表示他会写汉字

2. 看第二遍后用简单的话说出故事的主要内容

3. 朗读课文

五 语法 Grammar

（一）强调的表达法（1） The way to express emphasis (1)

疑问代词表示任指，并跟副词“都/也”搭配使用时，实际上是一种表示强调的方法。这种表达法强调无一例外。例如：

When interrogative pronouns indicates anyone, anything, any time or any place, these can be used together with the adverb “都” or “也” in a sentence. Such a sentence is used for emphasis on having no exception. For example:

（1）谁都认为这是件大事儿。

（2）明天你哪儿也别去，好好休息。

（3）没有什么地方他没去过。

（二）名词重叠 Noun reduplication

汉语里有一小部分名词可以重叠。单音节名词的重叠形式为AA，双音节名词的重叠形式为AABB。可重叠的名词，常见的单音节的有“人、家、村，天、日、月、年”，双音节的有“方面、花草、山水、年岁”等。例如：

In Chinese, only a small number of nouns can be reduplicated. The way a monosyllabic noun is reduplicated is AA, and that of a disyllabic noun is AABB. The frequently used nouns which can be reduplicated include monosyllabic nouns “人” “家” “村” “天” “日” “月” “年”, and disyllabic nouns “方面” “花草” “山水” “年岁” and so on. For example:

（1）这种小事儿，人人都做得了。

（2）他天天晚上听音乐。

（3）他生活和学习方方面面都做得很好。

Dì-wǔ kè
第五课 起名儿

一 课文 Text

王欢的妻子生了个女儿，都快满月了，还没有起名儿。一天晚饭后聊天儿时，王欢建议全家开个会讨论讨论。

会上，王欢的妻子强调说："名字最好是双音节的，好称呼。比如孩子她爸的名字是单音节的，叫他王欢吧，显得生分；叫他欢吧，太难听。"王欢的妹妹笑着说："嫂子不愧是语文老师，给孩子起名儿也讲究音节。"

王欢的妻子对公公婆婆是很尊敬的，她先征求他们的意见。王欢的父亲说："现在人民的生活全面达到了小康水平，叫王小康怎么样？"

王欢的妹妹第一个反对："爸，您不当官了，还想着国家大事，真是难得呀！可是，孩子长到五六十岁，别人还叫她小康，多不好！我建议叫王学艺，长大以后学艺术。"

王欢的母亲不同意："咱们家有你这么一个演员就够乱的了，再添一个演员，那可不得了！哎，要是个男孩子，可以叫王志强。"气氛一下子紧张起来，王欢的妹妹赶紧出来解围："妈，您说什么呀！男孩儿女孩儿都一样。"

王欢的母亲说完也有点儿后悔："我不是那个意思，我是说现在给女孩儿起名儿很难，再叫什么花呀草呀的不行了。"

于是，气氛又慢慢地缓和下来了。

这个会开了两个多小时，孩子的名字还是没定下来。最后，全家人一致决定，请方教授给孩子起名儿。

二 生词 New words

1. 起名儿	（动）	qǐmíngr	to give a name
2. 满月	（动）	mǎnyuè	a baby's completion of its first month of life
3. 讨论	（动）	tǎolùn	to discuss, to talk over
4. 音节	（名）	yīnjié	syllable
5. 称呼	（动）	chēnghu	to address, to call
6. 生分	（形）	shēngfen	not intimate enough, not well known to
7. 不愧	（副）	búkuì	to be worthy of, to deserve to be called
8. 语文	（名）	yǔwén	language and literature
9. 讲究	（动）	jiǎngjiu	to be particular about, to be too fastidious about
10. 公公	（名）	gōnggong	father-in-law, one's husband's father
11. 婆婆	（名）	pópo	mother-in-law, one's husband's mother
12. 尊敬	（动、形）	zūnjìng	to respect; respectful
13. 征求	（动）	zhēngqiú	to ask for, to seek, to solicit
14. 全面	（形）	quánmiàn	all-side, all-round, overall
15. 达到	（动）	dádào	to reach, to get to
16. 小康	（形）	xiǎokāng	fairly well-off, comparatively well-off
17. 反对	（动）	fǎnduì	to oppose, to object to
18. 官	（名）	guān	government official, officer
19. 难得	（形）	nándé	hard to come by, rare
20. 艺术	（名）	yìshù	art
21. 演员	（名）	yǎnyuán	actor or actress, performer
22. 乱	（形）	luàn	in disorder, in a mess
23. 一下子	（副）	yíxiàzi	all at once, all of a sudden
24. 赶紧	（副）	gǎnjǐn	in a haste, quickly
25. 解围	（动）	jiěwéi	to save sb. from embarrassment, to help sb. out of a predicament
26. 后悔	（动）	hòuhuǐ	to regret
27. 缓和	（形）	huǎnhé	mitigated, relaxed
28. 一致	（副）	yízhì	consistently, identically

补充词汇 Supplementary words

1. 继续	（动）	jìxù	to continue, to go on
2. 时代	（名）	shídài	age, era, times
3. 了不起	（形）	liǎobuqǐ	amazing, terrific, great
4. 周岁	（名）	zhōusuì	one full year of life
5. 高尚	（形）	gāoshàng	noble, lofty
6. 反映	（动）	fǎnyìng	to reflect
7. 同时	（名、连）	tóngshí	at the same time, meanwhile; moreover, besides
8. 道德	（名）	dàodé	morality, ethics
9. 重视	（动）	zhòngshì	to take sth. seriously, to attach importance to
10. 自从	（介）	zìcóng	since
自	（介）	zì	from
11. 至今	（副）	zhìjīn	so far, up to now
至	（动）	zhì	to, till
12. 盼望	（动）	pànwàng	to hope for, to look forward to
盼	（动）	pàn	to expect, to long for
13. 据说	（动）	jùshuō	it is said
14. 例如	（动）	lìrú	for example, such as
15. 往往	（副）	wǎngwǎng	often, frequently

专名 Proper nouns

1. 王小康	Wáng Xiǎokāng	name of a person
2. 王学艺	Wáng Xuéyì	name of a person
3. 王志强	Wáng Zhìqiáng	name of a person
4. 孔子	Kǒngzǐ	Confucius
5. 孔鲤	Kǒng Lǐ	son of Confucius

二 课堂练习 Exercises

（一）语音

1. 辨音辨调

yīnjié	音节	shēnfen	身份	bú guì	不贵
yíngjiē	迎接	shēngfen	生分	búkuì	不愧
bóbo	伯伯	jiǎngjiu	讲究	dádào	达到
pópo	婆婆	qiǎngqiú	强求	dàdào	大道
yīshù	医术	yízhì	一致	jīxù	积蓄
yìshù	艺术	yìzhí	一直	jìxù	继续
shídài	时代	quánmiàn	全面	fǎnduì	反对
shítài	时态	qiánmiàn	前面	fǎnkuì	反馈

2. 四音节声调

讨论问题	参加讨论	讲究卫生	讲究发音
讨论课文	开始讨论	讲究自由	讲究音节
讨论内容	进行讨论	讲究效果	讲究方法
讨论工作	继续讨论	讲究质量	讲究颜色
显得高兴	尊敬老师	继续工作	一致决定
显得亲切	尊敬老人	继续学习	一致同意
显得充分	尊敬领导	继续讨论	一致反对
显得生分	尊敬父母	继续上课	一致要求

3. 语调

（1）大内不愧是好学生，这次考试又是第一。

嫂子不愧是语文老师，给孩子起名儿也讲究音节。

妹妹不愧是当演员的，有名的电影她都知道。

爸爸不愧是当领导的，心里想的都是“人民人民”“小康小康”的。

（2）妈，您说什么呀！男孩儿女孩儿都一样。

爸，您说什么呀！男孩儿女孩儿都一样。

哥，你说什么呀！单音节双音节都一样。

姐，你说什么呀！单音节双音节都一样。

（3）我不是那个意思。

我不是那个想法。

我不是这个意思。

我不是这个想法。

（二）词语

1. 从本课生词表中选择合适的词语填空

（1）小张真________，他在运动会上得了四个第一。

（2）今天是我22________生日。

（3）您贵姓？怎么________？

（4）王欢的妻子是中学的________老师。

（5）京剧是中国的传统________。

（6）小王喜欢艺术，他以后希望成为一名电影________。

（7）方老师非常孝顺他的父母，是个________的好人。

（8）喜欢帮助别人是一种________的精神。

（9）文学要反映新________的新思想。

（10）我和彼得________到达北京。

（11）考试可以检查学生的学习情况，________也检查老师教的情况。

（12）大家都尊敬________高尚的人。

（13）老师和学生都非常________这次考试。

（14）你们有很大的进步，希望你们________努力，________更高的水平。

（15）我真________当时没听父母的话。

（16）时间快到了，________走吧。

（17）________前年他去了法国，________没给我打过电话。

（18）小时候的朋友很久没有联系，现在都________了。

（19）他说了几句笑话，气氛一下子________下来了。

（20）我们爱好和平，________战争。

（21）这个地区人民的生活已经达到了________水平。

（22）我们都________收到亲人的来信。

（23）这个房间太________了，咱们收拾一下吧。

（24）孩子都一周岁了，还没给他________。

2. 把下列句子的“据说”改成“据……说”

（1）据说这种药效果很好。

（2）据说明天刮大风。

（3）据说那个电影很有意思。

（4）据说地球有46亿年的历史了。

（5）据说小王结过三次婚。

（6）据说西方人认为13是不吉利的数字。

3. 用“例如”完成句子

（1）在中国，以前女人的名字多用花呀草呀的，________________。

（2）我很喜欢体育运动，______________________等，我都喜欢。

（3）中国有很多名胜古迹，______________________。

（4）我看过不少中国电影，______________________。

（5）艾米会唱很多中国歌曲，______________________。

（6）中国的水果很便宜，______________，比我们国家的便宜多了。

4. 用“往往”或“常常”填空

（1）他每天下午去图书馆看书，________一看就是两个小时。

（2）贝拉________一个人去旅行。

（3）希望你________来我家玩儿。

（4）他们________去饭馆儿吃饭。

（5）说话________能反映一个人的文化水平。

（6）你________去公园吗？

（7）考试前，我们________复习到深夜。

（8）不锻炼身体的人________容易感冒。

（三）功能会话：听后模仿

1. 询问职业

（1）A：贝拉的哥哥做什么工作？

B：他是大学老师。

（2）A：艾米的爸爸做什么工作？

B：他在美国一所大学教汉语。

（3）A：他是干什么的？

B：他是经商的。

（4）A：那个人是干什么的？

B：他是打篮球的。

2. 询问经历

（1）A：你以前吃过烤鸭吗？

B：我以前吃过烤鸭。

（2）A：你去过长城吗？

B：去过。

（3）A：你采访过孙教授吗？

B：采访过。

（4）A：你去过杭州吗？

B：去过，那儿青山绿水，风景可漂亮了。

3. 询问动量

（1）A：你去过几次长城？

B：两次。

（2）A：你采访过他几次？

B：我采访过他一次。

4. 询问比价

（1）A：今天美元对人民币的比价是多少？

B：100美元兑换644块人民币。

（2）A：今天英镑对人民币的比价是多少？

B：8.9。

5. 询问动作者（3）

（1）A：谁最后一个走的？

B：我最后一个走的。

（2）A：是谁把窗户打开的？

B：是我把窗户打开的。

（3）A：谁把那个老人背下了山？

B：王才把那个老人背下了山。

（4）A：你的词典让谁拿去了？

B：我的词典让艾米拿去了。

（5）A：贝拉的手机谁给取回来了？

B：山本给取回来了。

（6）A：你的照相机谁给弄坏了？

B：弟弟给弄坏了。

6. 询问动作对象（2）

（1）A：他把作业交给谁了？

B：他把作业交给孙老师了。

（2）A：你还要点儿什么吗？

B：不要了。

7. 要求证实（2）

（1）A：听说有的女人对丈夫管得很严，是这样吗？

B：是这样的。

（2）A：听说中秋节也叫团圆节，是吗？

B：汉族人把月圆看作团圆的象征，因此，中秋节也叫团圆节。

（3）A：学外语不能怕丢面子，怕丢面子就学不好外语，你说是吧？

B：的确是这样。

（4）A：这两位是你的父亲母亲，我没说错吧？

B：没错。

（5）A：怎么，把烟戒了？

B：对，我已经戒了半个月了。

四 家庭作业 Homework

（一）词语

用下列生词至少组成两个短语

（1）征求：________ ________　　（2）反对：________ ________

（3）继续：________ ________　　（4）重视：________ ________

（5）反映：________ ________　　（6）达到：________ ________

（7）后悔：________ ________　　（8）往往：________ ________

（二）阅读

起名儿的学问

中国人自古至今都很重视起名字。名字往往反映起名儿的人的文化水平和道德观念，也寄托（jìtuō，to place hope on）父母对孩子的理想和希望。

有文化的人起名字很讲究姓和名的声调。中国人的姓和名连在一起，姓在前，名在后。如果姓是第一、二、三声，名或名中的第一个音节多用第一、四声的字；如果姓是第四声，名或名中的第一个音节多用第一、二、三声的字。另外，如果兄弟姐妹的名是双音节的，第一个音节通常用相同的字，例如：刘志刚、刘志强、刘志勇、刘志琴。

中国人认为忠（zhōng，loyalty）、义（yì，justice）、礼、智（zhì，wisdom）、信是最高尚的道德，不少人给孩子起名字的时候都喜欢用上这些字，例如王忠、李义、马崇礼、周大智、于宏信等。大家都知道孔子吧，他有个儿子叫孔鲤。据说这个儿子出生的时候，国王送来了一条鲤鱼。国王送东西在当时是件很了不起的事情。为了纪念这件事，孔子给儿子起名叫孔鲤。

名字还能反映时代特点。比如建国、大庆、卫国、跃进、向东、振华、兴华等，一听就知道是什么时候出生的。以前有的人重男轻女，如果先生了一个女孩儿，就叫招弟、来弟、梦弟、盼弟等，盼望下一个生的是男孩儿。现在人们对生男生女的观念改变了，当然也就没有人再叫这些名字了。

1. 根据上下文猜词义

(1) 自古至今——

(2) 兄弟姐妹——

(3) 国王——

(4) 鲤鱼——

(5) 重男轻女——

2. 查词典，说说下列名字的意思

(1) 王忠——

(2) 李义——

(3) 马崇礼——

(4) 周大智——

（5）于宏信——

（6）张建国——

（7）孙大庆——

（8）陈卫国——

（9）宋国庆——

（10）赵跃进——

（11）郑文革——

（12）朱向东——

（13）常振华——

（14）杨兴华——

（15）方招弟——

（16）刘盼弟——

（三）写作

做一次街头调查（street survey），并写一篇调查报告。

街头调查内容：他们的名字，名字有什么特别的意思，谁给他们起的名字，等等。

五 语法 Grammar

宾语的成分 Components of object

宾语可由名词或名词性短语、代词、数量词、“的”字短语等充当，也可由形容词或形容词性短语、动词或动词性短语以及主谓短语等充当。例如：

The components which can act as objects are as follows: nouns, nominal phrases, pronouns, numeral classifier phrases, 的-phrases, adjectives, adjectival phrases, verbs, verbal phrases and subject-predicate phrases. For example:

（1）你天天看报吗？

（2）我也认识这个人。

（3）你在等谁？

（4）我只买两斤。

（5）这些书都是他借的。

（6）他最大的优点就是聪明。

（7）我认为不错。

（8）他最喜欢的运动是跑步。

（9）这个星期天，你打算去哪儿玩儿？

（10）我觉得这样做不太合适。

六 注释 Notes

孔子 Confucius

孔子（公元前551—公元前479），中国春秋时期鲁国（今山东省曲阜市东南）人，是中国历史上著名的思想家、政治家、教育家。孔子的学说对中国两千多年来的文化影响极大。

Confucius (B.C.551–B.C.479) born in Lu State (in the southeast of Qufu in Shandong Province today) in the Spring and Autumn Period in ancient China. He was a famous thinker, statesman and educator in the history of China, and his theories have a great influence upon the Chinese culture for more than 2000 years.

Dì-liù kè
第六课 北京的胡同

一 课文 Text

一天晚上，贝拉看了一个《逛胡同，看北京》的电视节目。主持人说："不去北京的胡同转转，就不能算是了解了北京。"这个节目引起了她对北京胡同的浓厚兴趣。

（第二天下午，贝拉来到方龙老师的办公室）

贝　拉：方老师，昨天晚上我看了一个介绍北京胡同的电视节目，有关这方面的知识，请您给我介绍介绍，好吗？

方　龙：好。胡同是城市里的小街道。中国古代和现在南方一些地方把它叫作"巷"，上海人把它叫作"里弄"，北京和北方其他一些城市把它称作"胡同"。大约从元朝起，就有了"胡同"这个词。经过元、明、清三个朝代，北京的胡同数目大大增加。老北京人说："有名儿胡同三百六，无名儿胡同似牛毛。"意思是说，一条一条的胡同数不清。

贝　拉：那到底有多少呢？

方　龙：我读过一本专门研究北京胡同的书，书上说北京城区有1320条胡同。

贝　拉：这么多呀！

方　龙：是啊，北京的胡同很有特色。墙连墙，房连房；正南正北，正东正西，排列整齐，好像灰色的波浪。千百条胡同有的长，有的短，有的宽，有的窄。名称也五花八门：有说明行业的，有以历史古迹得名的，也有用历史人物命名的。每条胡同都有自己的历史、自己的故事。它记录了北京的变迁，反映了北京经济文化的发展。有人说，胡同是北京一笔丰富的文化遗产，是一部百科全书，这话一点儿也不夸张。

贝　拉：怪不得那位电视主持人说不逛逛胡同，就不算了解北京呢。

二 生词 New words

1. 胡同	（名）	hútòng	lane, alley
2. 主持人	（名）	zhǔchírén	host, anchor
主持	（动）	zhǔchí	to host, to preside over, to chair
3. 引起	（动）	yǐnqǐ	to arouse, to provoke, to cause
4. 浓厚	（形）	nónghòu	strong, deep, thick
浓	（形）	nóng	(of degree or extent) great, strong, thick, dense
5. 有关	（介、动）	yǒuguān	about; to have sth. to do with, to relate to
6. 街道	（名）	jiēdào	street, road, way
7. 巷	（名）	xiàng	lane, alley
8. 里弄	（名）	lǐlòng	lanes and alleys
9. 称作	（动）	chēngzuò	to call, to name
称	（动）	chēng	to call
10. 从……起		cóng…qǐ	since, from
11. 数目	（名）	shùmù	number, amount
12. 似	（动）	sì	to be similar, to look like
13. 牛毛	（名）	niúmáo	ox hair, cowhair
毛	（名）	máo	hair, feather, fur, down
14. 正	（形）	zhèng	due, straight, upright
15. 排列	（动）	páiliè	to arrange, to put in order
16. 灰色	（名）	huīsè	gray
灰	（形）	huī	grey

17. 波浪	（名）	bōlàng	wave
18. 窄	（形）	zhǎi	narrow
19. 名称	（名）	míngchēng	name, title
20. 五花八门		wǔhuā-bāmén	of a wide variety, multifarious
21. 行业	（名）	hángyè	trade, profession
22. 以	（介）	yǐ	according to, because of, by
23. 得名	（动）	démíng	to nominate, to name, to be well-known
24. 人物	（名）	rénwù	figure, personage
25. 命名	（动）	mìngmíng	to name, to nominate
26. 记录	（动）	jìlù	to take notes, to record
27. 变迁	（动）	biànqiān	to change
28. 笔	（量）	bǐ	a measure word for a sum of money
29. 丰富	（形）	fēngfù	rich, abundant
30. 部	（量）	bù	a measure word for a book, a movie, etc.
31. 百科全书		bǎikē quánshū	encyclopedia
32. 夸张	（形）	kuāzhāng	exaggerated

补充词汇 Supplementary words

1. 由于	（介、连）	yóuyú	because of; because
2. 项目	（名）	xiàngmù	item, project, event
3. 新鲜	（形）	xīnxian	fresh
4. 改造	（动）	gǎizào	to reform, to change
5. 设备	（名）	shèbèi	equipment
6. 蔬菜	（名）	shūcài	vegetable
7. 风俗	（名）	fēngsú	custom
8. 亲自	（副）	qīnzì	in person, personally
9. 呼吸	（动）	hūxī	to breathe
呼	（动）	hū	to breathe out, to exhale
10. 奇特	（形）	qítè	peculiar, singular
11. 细	（形）	xì	thin, slender
12. 脏	（形）	zāng	dirty
13. 感兴趣		gǎn xìngqù	to be interested in
14. 网络	（名）	wǎngluò	network

15. 越来越……		yuè lái yuè…	more and more
16. 作用	（名）	zuòyòng	effect, function
17. 加	（动）	jiā	to add, to plus
18. 井	（名）	jǐng	well

专名 Proper nouns

1. 元朝	Yuáncháo	Yuan Dynasty
2. 明（朝）	Míng (cháo)	Ming Dynasty
3. 清（朝）	Qīng (cháo)	Qing Dynasty

二 课堂练习 Exercises

（一）语音

1. 辨音辨调

hútòng	胡同	hányè	寒夜	yóuyú	由于
huódòng	活动	hángyè	行业	yōuyù	忧郁
xiàngmù	项目	fēnfu	吩咐	xìnxiāng	信箱
xiàngmào	相貌	fēngfù	丰富	xīnxian	新鲜

2. 四音节声调

主持晚会	改造技术	新鲜空气	食品丰富
主持讨论	改造设备	新鲜猪肉	产品丰富
主持考试	改造社会	新鲜鸡蛋	展品丰富
主持比赛	改造世界	新鲜蔬菜	水果丰富

3. 语调

（1）那到底有多少呢？

那到底有多远呢？

那到底有多大呢？

那到底有多重呢？

（2）这么多呀！

这么大呀！

这么高哇！

这么长啊！

（二）词语

1. 连线并朗读

一条	整齐
引起	奇特
有关	胡同
排列	空气
文化	兴趣
风俗	人物
内容	项目
亲自	单位
新鲜	参加
主要	困难
旅游	丰富
呼吸	遗产

2. 从本课生词表中选择合适的词语填空

（1）这个城市的________没有北京的宽，都很________。

（2）小刘说的问题很重要，________了大家的注意。

（3）北京胡同的________太多了，很难数清楚。

（4）我们还邀请了学校的________领导参加今天的晚会。

（5）这条胡同是以一个历史人物的名字________的。

(6) 白老师做的面条儿细________头发。

(7) 外面下起了牛________细雨。

(8) 这本小说记录了这个城市的________。

(9) 这个班里充满了________的学习气氛。

(10) 陈平想当电视节目________。

(11) 你说得太________了！面条儿怎么可能像头发那么细？

(12) 你的衣服________了，脱下来洗洗吧。

(13) 近现代很多著名的历史________都出自湖南省。

(14) 这篇文章的内容非常________。

(15) 那个病人________越来越困难了。

(16) 马校长________把我们送到火车站。

(17) 我对体育不________，什么运动________也没参加。

(18) 这些水果很________，也不太贵。

(19) 网络在人民生活中起着越来越大的________。

(20) 这个城市应该________交通，加宽街道，修建立交桥。

3. 读下列句子，注意“加”的用法

(1) A：二加三得几？

B：二加三得五。

(2) A：四十加六十得多少？

B：四十加六十得一百。

(3) A：你把这个数字加上了吗？

B：我把这个数字加上了。

(4) 你要是住那个房间得加钱。

(5) 你的汽车该加油了。

(6) 我们班又加了两个学生。

(7) 这条道太窄了，应该加宽。

(8) 你这样做加大了困难。

（三）句型

1. 替换

（1）操场上一个人也没有。

墙上	画儿（张）
路上	汽车（辆）
书架上	书（本）
教室里	学生（个）
钱包里	钱（块）
这篇课文（里）	生词（个）
这个村子（里）	井（口）
这间房子（里）	窗户（个）

（2）世界公园我一次也没去过。

外国电影	部	看
外文小说	本	读
百科全书	本	买
广东菜	次	吃
这种茶	次	喝
这件衣服	次	穿
这台电脑	次	用
北京的胡同	次	逛

（3）这话一点儿也不夸张。

我	后悔
小王	聪明
这个孩子	傻
这个电影	好看
那个售货员	热情
这儿的夏天	热
这儿的冬天	冷
今年的春节	热闹

(4) 北京的胡同有的长，有的短。

这个城市的街道	宽	窄
这些房子	高	矮
这些树	粗	细
这些苹果	大	小
孩子们的小手	干净	脏
这些练习	难	容易
这些服务员	热情	不热情
这些文章	重要	不重要

(5) 北京人把小的街道称作胡同。

南方人	胡同	巷或小巷
上海人	胡同	里弄或弄堂
中国人	婚姻介绍人	红娘
西方人	长城	伟大的墙
西方人	颐和园	夏宫
人们	故宫	紫禁城（Zǐjìnchéng）

2. 选择正确的回答

(1) 操场上怎么一个人也没有？ (　　)

(2) 你常看外国电影吧？ (　　)

(3) 这儿的冬天是不是很冷？ (　　)

(4) 你说的是不是太夸张了？ (　　)

(5) 这篇课文生词多吗？ (　　)

(6) 你害怕了吧？ (　　)

(7) 房子周围有树吗？ (　　)

(8) 你怎么一口咖啡也不喝？ (　　)

a. 我说的一点儿也不夸张。

b. 我一点儿也不害怕。

c. 这儿的冬天一点儿也不冷。

d. 都去礼堂看电影去了。

e. 房子周围一棵树也没有。

f. 这篇课文一个生词也没有。

g. 外国电影我一部也没看过。

h. 我不喜欢苦的味道。

四 家庭作业 Homework

（一）词语

1. 用“由于”完成句子

（1）____________，我没参加比赛。

（2）____________，我的考试成绩不太好。

（3）____________，我常常感冒。

（4）____________，我得马上回国。

（5）____________，所以我们迟到了。

（6）____________，因此取得了好成绩。

2. 用“越来越……”完成句子

（1）现在是11月了，天气____________。

（2）你的女儿__________________。

（3）那些老人每天运动，又唱歌又跳舞，好像__________________。

（4）我们学的生词____________。

（5）丁兰对书法__________________。

（6）这里的变化____________。

（二）阅读

逛胡同

“胡同”这个词，据说是从蒙古语中借过来的，本义是水井，借过来以后表示有水井的小街道。水井在城市人民的生活中起着非常重要的作用。过去，北京的胡同里一般都有水井，有的一口，有的两口，还有的三口四口。现在自来水代替了井水，所以水井就很难见到了。

北京城区和近郊过去大约有3000条胡同，由于房屋和街道的改造，现在只有大约1000多条了。再过些年，北京的胡同可能还会减少。要想了解北京胡同现在的状况和历史的变迁，了解北京人的生活和风俗习惯，就得亲自去胡同转转，看看胡同里的四合院儿，跟住在那里的老北京人聊聊。

北京有些旅游公司开设了“胡同游”的项目。如果你对北京的胡同感兴趣，就坐上三轮车去逛逛吧。北京的胡同有的长，有的短，有的宽，有的窄，有的笔直笔直，有的弯弯曲曲。坐在三轮车上一边参观，一边听介绍，既呼吸新鲜空气，又增长知识，真是一种难得的乐趣。

1. 根据上下文猜词义

（1）本义——

（2）自来水——

（3）井水——

（4）开设——

（5）三轮车——

（6）笔直——

（7）乐趣——

2. 读后回答

（1）“胡同”这个词是从哪儿来的？本义是什么？

（2）现在为什么很难见到水井了？

（3）北京的胡同为什么越来越少？

（4）参观胡同可以了解什么？

（5）北京有些旅游公司开设了什么项目？

（6）为什么说坐三轮车逛胡同是一种难得的乐趣？

3. 朗读课文

五 语法 Grammar

（一）强调的表达法（2） The way to express emphasis (2)

“一 + 量词（ + 名词）+ 也/都 + 不/没 + 形容词/动词”这种格式用来表示强调。这种表达法是通过对下限的否定来否定总体，强调完全否定。例如：

The construction “一 + classifier (+ noun) + 也/都 + 不/没 + adjective/verb” is used for emphasis, which negates the minimum in order to negate the entirety. It stresses a complete negation. For example:

（1）操场上一个人也没有。

（2）到这儿以后，我一部电影也没看过。

（3）世界公园我一次都没去过。

（4）这话一点儿也不夸张。

（二）数量词重叠 Numeral classifier phrase reduplication

数词与量词构成的数量词可以重叠。

Numeral classifier phrases can be reduplicated.

数词为“一”时，可与物量词一起重叠，也可与动量词一起重叠。

When the numeral is “一”, it can be reduplicated together either with a substance measure word or with an action measure word.

“一”与物量词一起重叠时，可做定语，也可做状语。做定语时，强调事物接连不断，数量多；做状语时，强调以个体为单位依次进行某种活动。例如：

When “一” and a substance measure word are reduplicated together, they can act as an attributive or adverbial. When acting as an attributive, they emphasize rapid succession and abundance. When used as an adverbial, they stress the idea that individuals proceed in proper order in a certain activity. For example:

（1）一条一条的胡同数不清。

（2）他们一个一个地进去了。

“一”与动量词一起重叠时，一般做状语，多强调连续不断地进行某种活动。例如：

When “一” and an action measure word are reduplicated together, they usually act as an adverbial, emphasizing successive progression of a certain activity. For example:

（3）我一遍一遍地念课文。

（4）他一次一次地喊我。

大于“一”的数词与物量词一起重叠时，只能做状语，强调分组进行某种活动。例如：

When a numeral which is more than “一” is reduplicated together with a substance measure word, they can only act as an adverbial, stressing taking part in a certain activity in groups. For example:

（5）你们两个两个地进去！

（6）你们三个三个地讨论这些问题。

（7）你们五个五个地排列整齐！

六 附录 Appendix

中国历史年代简表

A Brief Chinese Chronology

夏 Xià	约公元前 2070—前 1600 年
商 Shāng	公元前 1600—前 1046 年

续表

西周 Xī Zhōu		公元前 1046—前 771 年
东周 Dōng Zhōu	春秋 Chūnqiū	公元前 770 年—前 476 年
	战国 Zhànguó	公元前 475 年—前 221 年
秦 Qín		公元前 221 年—前 206 年
汉 Hàn	西汉 Xī Hàn	公元前 206 年—25 年
	东汉 Dōng Hàn	公元 25 年—220 年
三国（魏、蜀、吴） Sān Guó（Wèi、Shǔ、Wú）		公元 220 年—280 年
晋 Jìn	西晋 Xī Jìn	公元 265 年—317 年
	东晋 Dōng Jìn	公元 317 年—420 年
南北朝 Nán-Běi Cháo		公元 420 年—589 年
隋 Suí		公元 581 年—618 年
唐 Táng		公元 618 年—907 年
五代 Wǔ Dài		公元 907 年—960 年
宋 Sòng	北宋 Běi Sòng	公元 960 年—1127 年
	南宋 Nán Sòng	公元 1127 年—1279 年
辽 Liáo		公元 907 年—1125 年

续表

西夏 Xī Xià	公元1038年—1227年
金 Jīn	公元1115年—1234年
元 Yuán	公元1206年—1368年
明 Míng	公元1368年—1644年
清 Qīng	公元1616年—1911年

Dì-qī kè

第七课 这茶味道不错

一 课文 Text

（一）

（丁兰、大内上子和金汉成在茶馆儿里喝茶）

大　内：这茶味道不错。连我这很少喝茶的人也喝了好几杯。

金汉成：这就是普通的茉莉花茶，质量一般，一斤不超过100块钱。

大　内：看不出来，你对中国茶还有点儿研究呢。

金汉成：研究谈不上。要说中国的名茶，我差不多都品尝过。

丁　兰：是吗？你都喝过哪些名茶？

金汉成：杭州的龙井、苏州的碧螺春、安徽黄山的毛峰、福建的乌龙茶、云南的红茶，等等，我都尝过。

丁　兰：你简直成了饮茶专家了。

金汉成：不敢当。不过，我确实爱读有关茶文化的书。记得有一篇文章说，茶的味道跟沏茶的水有很大关系。最好的水是山泉，其次是井水，城里的自来水就差点儿。

丁　兰：你们去过我的家乡杭州吗？坐在西湖的茶园里，用虎跑泉的水沏一杯龙井茶，那真是人生一大享受。

大　内：一个朋友对我说，虎跑泉的水是上等矿泉水，硬币能浮在水面上不下沉。

金汉成：是吗？那下个月我就去杭州，游西湖，喝龙井，再尝尝那儿的醋鱼。

大　内：每天上课你都带着一杯茶水，那是什么好茶？

金汉成：我喝的茶对健康有好处。

丁　兰：什么好处？

金汉成：减肥。

（二）

茶最早产于中国。据说，中国人种植茶树已有4000多年的历史了。

中国人喜欢喝茶，而且已经成为一种传统的生活习惯。喝茶不仅是为了解渴，还因为茶有多种功能。饭后喝杯茶，可以助消化；困了喝杯茶，可以提精神。此外，喝茶还可以解毒，补充人体的维生素C。

中国地方大，人多，各地区、各民族喝茶的习惯不太一样。北方人一般爱喝花茶，南方人大多喜欢喝绿茶。如果去西藏旅游，当地人会为你敬上一碗酥油茶。如果在内蒙古牧民家里做客，他们会给你端来一杯又咸又香的奶茶。

早在1500年以前，中国的茶叶就往国外出口了。很多国家语言里的“茶”都是从汉语的“茶”或者“茶叶”音译过去的。例如，日语的“茶”字跟汉语的“茶”字一样，英语的“tea”是从福建话里“茶”的发音音译过去的。

二 生词 New words

1. 茶馆儿	（名）	cháguǎnr	teahouse
2. 茉莉花茶	（名）	mòlìhuāchá	jasmine tea
茉莉花	（名）	mòlìhuā	jasmine
3. 超过	（动）	chāoguò	to exceed, to surpass
4. 龙井	（名）	lóngjǐng	a famous green tea produced in Hangzhou, Dragon well tea
5. 碧螺春	（名）	bìluóchūn	a special brand of tea, Biluochun
6. 毛峰	（名）	máofēng	Huang Shan Mao Feng tea, yellow mountain fuzz tip
7. 简直	（副）	jiǎnzhí	simply, at all
8. 饮茶	（动）	yǐnchá	to drink tea

9. 专家	（名）	zhuānjiā	expert, specialist
10. 山泉	（名）	shānquán	mountain spring
泉	（名）	quán	spring
11. 其次	（代）	qícì	next, secondly, then
12. 自来水	（名）	zìláishuǐ	tap-water, running water
13. 茶园	（名）	cháyuán	tea plantation
14. 享受	（动）	xiǎngshòu	to enjoy
15. 上等	（形）	shàngděng	first-class, first-rate
16. 矿泉水	（名）	kuàngquánshuǐ	mineral water
17. 硬币	（名）	yìngbì	coin, specie
硬	（形）	yìng	hard, tough, stiff
18. 浮	（动）	fú	to float
19. 水面	（名）	shuǐmiàn	the surface of the water
面	（名）	miàn	surface, top
20. 沉	（动）	chén	to sink
21. 于	（介）	yú	from, in
22. 种植	（动）	zhòngzhí	to plant, to cultivate, to grow
23. 功能	（名）	gōngnéng	function
24. 消化	（动）	xiāohuà	to digest
25. 解毒	（动）	jiědú	to detoxicate, to relieve internal heat or fever
毒	（名）	dú	poison
26. 补充	（动）	bǔchōng	to supply, to replenish
27. 人体	（名）	réntǐ	human body
28. 维生素	（名）	wéishēngsù	vitamin
29. 花茶	（名）	huāchá	scented tea
30. 敬	（动）	jìng	to offer politely
31. 酥油茶	（名）	sūyóuchá	buttered tea
酥油	（名）	sūyóu	butter
32. 牧民	（名）	mùmín	herdsman
33. 奶茶	（名）	nǎichá	tea with milk, milky tea
34. 出口	（动）	chūkǒu	to export
35. 音译	（动）	yīnyì	to transliterate

补充词汇　Supplementary words

1. 总之	（连）	zǒngzhī	in a word, in short, in brief
2. 信息	（名）	xìnxī	information
3. 医学	（名）	yīxué	medical science
4. 缺少	（动）	quēshǎo	to lack, to be short of
5. 交流	（动）	jiāoliú	to exchange, to interflow
6. 法学	（名）	fǎxué	the science of law
7. 洽谈	（动）	qiàtán	to talk over with, to make arrangements with
8. 曲艺	（名）	qǔyì	Chinese folk art forms
9. 场所	（名）	chǎngsuǒ	place, arena
10. 壶	（名）	hú	pot, kettle
11. 聚会	（动）	jùhuì	to get together, to meet
12. 老百姓	（名）	lǎobǎixìng	ordinary people, common people

专名　Proper nouns

1. 安徽	Ānhuī	name of a province
2. 黄山	Huáng Shān	Huangshan Mountain
3. 福建	Fújiàn	name of a province
4. 云南	Yúnnán	name of a province
5. 虎跑泉	Hǔpǎo Quán	Hupao Spring, Tiger-running Spring
6. 西藏	Xīzàng	Tibet
7. 内蒙古	Nèiměnggǔ	Inner Mongolia
8. 泰国	Tàiguó	Thailand
9. 老舍	Lǎo Shě	name of a famous writer

二 课堂练习 Exercises

（一）语音

1. 辨音辨调

huāchá	花茶	měilì	美丽	zhuānjiā	专家
hóngchá	红茶	mòlì	茉莉	zhuāngjia	庄稼

xiàohua	笑话	zōngzhǐ	宗旨	xìnxī	信息
xiāohuà	消化	zǒngzhī	总之	xìnxīn	信心

2. 四音节声调

医学专家	产于中国	缺少经验	交流经验
哲学专家	产于韩国	缺少知识	交流情况
法学专家	产于美国	缺少设备	交流文化
数学专家	产于泰国	缺少技术	交流技术

（二）词语

1. 连线并朗读

茉莉	水面
饮茶	幸福
上等	花茶
享受	福建
浮在	专家
产于	艺术家
解	矿泉水
多种	节目
洽谈	功能
交流	生意
人民	毒
曲艺	信息

2. 从本课生词表中选择合适的词语填空

（1）我们的校长是一位教育________。

（2）黄山毛峰是________绿茶。

（3）这里的风景________太美了。

(4) 饭后吃水果可以帮助________。

(5) 我最喜欢大熊猫，________是猴子。

(6) 饭后听听音乐是人生的一大________。

(7) 维生素C是人体不可________的。

(8) 公园是人们休息的________。

(9) 这台电脑有多种________。

(10) 水面上________着一只小船。

(11) 汉语里很多名称是________的，例如“可口可乐”“沙发”等。

(12) 他们的产品大部分________国外。

(13) 他正在跟客人________生意。

(14) ________们生活在大草原上，他们喜欢喝________。

(15) 在中国常能看到孩子们给国旗________礼。

(16) 我很喜欢看________节目。

(17) 老师们常常________教学经验。

(18) 这________茶是刚沏的。

(三) 句型

替换

(1) 连我这<u>很少喝茶</u>的人也<u>喝了好几杯</u>。

很少喝花茶	喝了好几杯
很少喝绿茶	喝了几杯
很少喝咖啡	喝了一杯
很少喝酒	喝了一杯
很少看京剧	看了好几场
很少打扑克	打了半天
很少打麻将	打了半天
不会游泳	下水了

不喜欢打球	参加比赛了
没学过几天英语	听懂了

（2）他连“你好”都不会说。

简单的句子	听不懂
简单的句子	说不对
拼音	不会念
一个字	不会写
小学	没上过
北京	没去过
火车	没坐过
一个生词	没记住
一块钱	没有
一块钱	没有了

四 家庭作业 Homework

（一）词语

完成句子

（1）茶最早产于________________。

（2）这种水果产于________________。

（3）艾米生于________________。

（4）老王毕业于________________。

（5）我们学校位于________________。

（6）这个学校建于________________。

（二）阅读

去茶馆儿学汉语

你一定进过大饭店，去过咖啡厅，也可能去过酒吧，不知道你进过中国的茶馆儿没有？

在中国，几乎每个城镇都有茶馆儿，特别是在南方的一些省市。那里的茶馆儿很多，城市大街上有茶馆儿，小巷里有茶馆儿，公园里有茶馆儿，就连郊外的农村也有茶馆儿。最近几年，一些城市还新建了一些高级茶厅、音乐茶座。当地的人们都有坐茶馆儿的习惯。有些人一清早就到茶馆儿喝茶，有些人下班后到那里坐上两三个小时，或读书看报，或一边喝茶一边聊天儿。到了节假日，朋友们也常常在茶馆儿里聚会，或洽谈生意，或讨论问题，有些茶馆儿还经常举办各种文化活动。总之，茶馆儿不仅是老百姓生活中不可缺少的休息场所，也是人们交流信息的一个重要场所，同时，也为国内外游客提供了一个了解当地民俗民情的好地方。

北京的茶馆儿也不少。其中最有名的，要算前门附近的"老舍茶馆"。这是以人民艺术家老舍先生的名字命名的茶馆儿。当客人走进"老舍茶馆"，服务员会马上端来一壶热茶和几种北京风味的小吃，客人一边喝着、吃着，一边观看传统的京剧和曲艺节目。现在，"老舍茶馆"已经成为一处名胜，它每天都吸引着中外客人来这儿参观。

如果你有时间，可以去茶馆儿里坐坐。你会更多地了解到北京的民俗，感受到北京人传统的文化气氛。你会在那里听到不少新闻，交更多的朋友。茶馆儿还是学习汉语的第二课堂呢。不信，你去一次试试。

1. 选出课文中没提到的内容

（1）哪些地方有茶馆儿？

A. 城市大街上　　B. 小巷里

C. 学校里　　D. 公园里

（2）人们什么时候去茶馆儿？

A. 早上　　B. 午饭后

C. 下班后　　D. 节假日

（3）人们去茶馆儿做什么？

A. 喝茶、聊天儿　　B. 聚会

C. 看书看报　　D. 开会

（4）在“老舍茶馆”除了喝茶以外还有什么活动？

A. 吃北京风味的小吃　　B. 观看京剧

C. 观看曲艺节目　　D. 洽谈生意、讨论问题

2. 回答问题

跟朋友聚会你会去咖啡厅还是茶馆儿？你觉得咖啡厅和茶馆儿有什么不同？

五 语法 Grammar

（一）处所补语　Locative complement

由介词“于”及其宾语组成的介宾短语可做处所补语。例如：

A prepositional phrase composed of the preposition “于” and its object can act as a locative complement. For example:

（1）茶最早产于哪个国家？

（2）他出生于一个大城市。

（3）他毕业于北京大学。

注意：这种处所补语限用于书面语和较正式的口语，非正式的口语一般用“是（在/从）……的”格式。例如：

Point for attention: This kind of complement is only used in written language or in formal circumstances. In spoken language under informal circumstances, the construction “是（在/从）……的” is used instead. For example:

（4）茶最早是哪个国家生产的？

（5）他是（在）大城市出生的。

（6）他是（从）北京大学毕业的。

（二）强调的表达法（3） The way to express emphasis (3)

“连……也/都……”格式用来表示强调。这种表达法是通过举出最突出、最极端的例子来概括总体，或通过对上限的肯定来肯定总体，或通过对下限的否定来否定总体，强调完全肯定或完全否定或不合常情。例如：

The construction “连……也/都……” is used to express emphasis. The emphasis is achieved by giving the most striking and extreme example to imply the inclusion of entirety, by affirming the maximum so as to affirm the entirety, or by negating the minimum in order to negate the entirety. In such a construction, the emphasis is placed on complete affirmation, complete negation, or contradiction to common sense. For example:

（1）这茶味道不错，连我这很少喝茶的人也喝了好几杯。（完全肯定）

（2）这次比赛，连校领导都参加了。（完全肯定）

（3）他连小学都没上过。（完全否定）

（4）他的奶奶一辈子连汽车也没坐过。（完全否定）

（5）这个人真怪，连肉都不吃！（不合常情）

（6）雨下得这么大，他连伞都不带就走了。（不合常情）

六 附录 Appendix

中国的少数民族

Ethnic Minorities in China

阿昌族	Āchāngzú	白族	Báizú
保安族	Bǎo'ānzú	布朗族	Bùlǎngzú
布依族	Bùyīzú	朝鲜族	Cháoxiǎnzú
达斡尔族	Dáwò'ěrzú	傣族	Dǎizú
德昂族	Dé'ángzú	东乡族	Dōngxiāngzú

续表

侗族	Dòngzú	独龙族	Dúlóngzú
俄罗斯族	Éluósīzú	鄂伦春族	Èlúnchūnzú
鄂温克族	Èwēnkèzú	高山族	Gāoshānzú
仡佬族	Gēlǎozú	哈尼族	Hānízú
哈萨克族	Hāsàkèzú	赫哲族	Hèzhézú
回族	Huízú	基诺族	Jīnuòzú
京族	Jīngzú	景颇族	Jǐngpōzú
柯尔克孜族	Kē'ěrkèzīzú	拉祜族	Lāhùzú
黎族	Lízú	傈僳族	Lìsùzú
珞巴族	Luòbāzú	满族	Mǎnzú
毛南族	Máonánzú	门巴族	Ménbāzú
蒙古族	Měnggǔzú	苗族	Miáozú
仫佬族	Mùlǎozú	纳西族	Nàxīzú
怒族	Nùzú	普米族	Pǔmǐzú
羌族	Qiāngzú	撒拉族	Sālāzú
畲族	Shēzú	水族	Shuǐzú
塔吉克族	Tǎjíkèzú	塔塔尔族	Tǎtǎ'ěrzú
土家族	Tǔjiāzú	土族	Tǔzú
佤族	Wǎzú	维吾尔族	Wéiwú'ěrzú
乌孜别克族	Wūzībiékèzú	锡伯族	Xībózú
瑶族	Yáozú	彝族	Yízú
裕固族	Yùgùzú	藏族	Zàngzú
壮族	Zhuàngzú		

Dì-bā kè 第八课 写给朋友的一封电子邮件

一 课文 Text

亲爱的依丽拉：

你好！

昨天刚旅游回来，今天上午就给你写了这封邮件。

中国的国庆节期间，我去山西大同旅游了。

9月29日夜里，我登上了开往大同的火车。在火车上，我认识了一个学化学的中国大学生，她叫宋英。我真感谢宋英，她是我的旅伴，也是我的向导。

第二天上午，我们来到了大同市西面15公里处的武周山。我亲眼看到了闻名中外的云冈石窟。53座大大小小的石窟东西排列，长约1公里。这里共有50000多个石雕，是中国最大的石雕群之一。

宋英告诉我，云冈石窟开凿于公元5世纪，整个石窟的完成大约用了60年的时间。1000多年来，一些石雕因为不断受到自然和人为的破坏而出现残缺。中华人民共和国成立以后，这座珍贵的艺术宝库才得到了较好的保护。

我们一个洞窟一个洞窟地参观，看得很仔细。洞窟里的佛像有的坐着，有的卧着，有的跪着。我把那些保存完好的佛像都拍摄了下来。这不仅是为了留念，而且也是为了你。你不是喜欢美术和雕塑吗？

我把这些石窟的照片都放在附件里了，一起发给你。你打开看看，希望这

些照片能启发你的创作灵感。对了，昨天晚上我的好朋友丁兰来找我玩儿，她看了这些照片，连声称赞我的拍照技术。你看我的拍照技术是不是进步了？

好了，就写到这儿，下次旅游以后再给你去信。

你的好友　贝拉

10月3日

二 生词 New words

1. 化学	（名）	huàxué	chemistry
2. 旅伴	（名）	lǚbàn	fellow traveller, travelling companion
3. 向导	（名）	xiàngdǎo	guide
4. 亲眼	（副）	qīnyǎn	with one's own eyes, personally
5. 石窟	（名）	shíkū	rock cave, grotto
6. 约	（副）	yuē	about, around, approximately
7. 石雕	（名）	shídiāo	carved stone
8. 开凿	（动）	kāizáo	to dig, to cut
9. 公元	（名）	gōngyuán	the Christian era
10. 自然	（名、形）	zìrán	nature; natural
11. 人为	（形）	rénwéi	man-made, artificial
为	（动）	wéi	to do, to act
12. 破坏	（动）	pòhuài	to destroy, to damage
13. 出现	（动）	chūxiàn	to appear, to arise
14. 残缺	（动）	cánquē	to be incomplete
15. 成立	（动）	chénglì	to found, to establish
16. 宝库	（名）	bǎokù	treasure-house, treasury
17. 保护	（动）	bǎohù	to protect, to defend
18. 洞窟	（名）	dòngkū	cavern
洞	（名）	dòng	hole, cave
19. 仔细	（形）	zǐxì	careful
20. 佛像	（名）	fóxiàng	figure of the Buddha, image of the Buddha
佛	（名）	fó	the Buddha

21. 卧	（动）	wò	to lie
22. 跪	（动）	guì	to kneel, to go down on one's knees
23. 完好	（形）	wánhǎo	intact, whole, in good condition
24. 拍摄	（动）	pāishè	to take (a picture), to shoot
25. 留念	（动）	liúniàn	to keep or accept as a souvenir
26. 美术	（名）	měishù	the fine arts, painting
27. 雕塑	（名）	diāosù	sculpture
28. 启发	（动）	qǐfā	to illuminate, to enlighten, to inspire
29. 创作	（动）	chuàngzuò	to create, to produce
30. 灵感	（名）	línggǎn	inspiration
31. 称赞	（动）	chēngzàn	to praise
32. 拍照	（动）	pāizhào	to take a picture
33. 技术	（名）	jìshù	skill, technique

补充词汇 Supplementary words

1. 情景	（名）	qíngjǐng	scene, sight, circumstances
2. 平均	（动）	píngjūn	to average
3. 收入	（名）	shōurù	income
4. 欢乐	（形）	huānlè	happy, joyous
5. 宴会	（名）	yànhuì	banquet, dinner party
6. 弹	（动）	tán	to play, to pluck
7. 琴	（名）	qín	a general name for certain musical instrument
8. 待	（动）	dāi	to stay
9. 埋	（动）	mái	to bury, to cover
10. 沙子	（名）	shāzi	sand, grit
11. 部位	（名）	bùwèi	place, position, location
12. 偏偏	（副）	piānpiān	deliberately, just, only
偏	（副）	piān	deliberately, just, only
13. 串	（量）	chuàn	bunch, a measure word for keys, grapes, etc.
14. 哈密瓜	（名）	hāmìguā	Hami melon

专名 Proper nouns

1. 依丽拉	Yīlìlā	name of a person
2. 国庆节	Guóqìngjié	National Day
3. 山西	Shānxī	name of a province
4. 大同	Dàtóng	name of a city in Shanxi Province
5. 宋英	Sòng Yīng	name of a person
6. 武周山	Wǔzhōu Shān	Wuzhou Mountain
7. 云冈石窟	Yúngāng Shíkū	Yungang Grottoes
8. 中华人民共和国	Zhōnghuá Rénmín Gònghéguó	the People's Republic of China
9. 吐鲁番	Tǔlǔfān	name of a place, Turpan

二 课堂练习 Exercises

（一）语音

1. 辨音辨调

gōngyuán	公元	pòhuài	破坏	chénglì	成立
guǒyuán	果园	pòhài	迫害	chénliè	陈列
bǎokù	宝库	chēzhàn	车站	qīngjìng	清静
bǎohù	保护	chēngzàn	称赞	qíngjǐng	情景

2. 四音节声调

破坏建筑	保护环境	听得仔细	平均长度
破坏道路	保护孩子	谈得仔细	平均年龄
破坏纪律	保护母亲	想得仔细	平均成绩
破坏规定	保护眼睛	看得仔细	平均收入

（二）词语

1. 连线并朗读

说得	宝库
受到	石窟
残缺	电影
艺术	破坏
拍摄	自然
保存	不全
开凿	完好
称赞	情景
举行	宴会
平均	学生
欢乐	奇迹
出现	气温

2. 从本课生词表中选择合适的词语填空

（1）这个故事发生在________10世纪。

（2）最近电视上________了一些新的主持人。

（3）这条河长________10公里。

（4）这个国家是去年________的。

（5）你拍照的________怎么样？

（6）工人们正在________山洞，修建铁路。

（7）这些佛像________不全了，好像是________破坏的。

（8）大内从小喜欢________，她画的画儿可好看了。

（9）看了山本________的照片，大家都________他的拍照技术。

（10）我们班同学的________年龄是23岁。

（11）人们都很重视________这些著名的文化遗产。

（12）中国大使馆举行了一个________庆祝国庆节。

（13）晚会上同学们有的________琴，有的唱歌。

（14）你打算在这儿________几天？

（15）我常常想起第一次离开家的________。

（16）孩子们把腿________在沙子里。

（17）孩子太小，需要母亲的________。

（18）老师把考试的要求说得很________。

（19）你的发音________和发音方法不对。

（20）在国庆假期几天里大家都过得很快乐，________只有彼得不高兴。

（三）句型

1. 替换

（1）我们一个洞窟一个洞窟地参观。

服务员	一个房间	打扫
大夫们	一个病房	检查
艾米	一个词	写
大内	一个句子	练习
同学们	一篇课文	复习
老师	一个问题	解释
我们	一个人	进去
他们	一个商店	逛
贝拉	一双鞋	试
工人们	一条路	修

（2）饭要一口一口地吃。

事儿	一件	做
生词	一个	记
录音	一段	听
练习	一个	做
衣服	一件	洗

问题	一个	讨论
错误	一个	改正
小说	一本	看
文章	一篇	写
节目	一个	表演

2. 完成句子

(1) 老舍生于＿＿＿＿＿＿＿＿，死于＿＿＿＿＿＿＿＿。

(2) 小宋毕业于＿＿＿＿＿＿＿＿。

(3) 这所医院建于＿＿＿＿＿＿＿＿。

(4) 这个国家成立于＿＿＿＿＿＿＿＿。

(5) 云冈石窟开凿于＿＿＿＿＿＿＿＿。

(6) 这种病出现于＿＿＿＿＿＿＿＿。

四 家庭作业 Homework

(一) 词语

用下列生词至少组成两个短语

(1) 自然：＿＿＿＿ ＿＿＿＿　　(2) 破坏：＿＿＿＿ ＿＿＿＿

(3) 成立：＿＿＿＿ ＿＿＿＿　　(4) 保护：＿＿＿＿ ＿＿＿＿

(5) 仔细：＿＿＿＿ ＿＿＿＿　　(6) 拍摄：＿＿＿＿ ＿＿＿＿

(7) 称赞：＿＿＿＿ ＿＿＿＿　　(8) 出现：＿＿＿＿ ＿＿＿＿

(9) 卧：＿＿＿＿ ＿＿＿＿　　(10) 跪：＿＿＿＿ ＿＿＿＿

(11) 待：＿＿＿＿ ＿＿＿＿　　(12) 埋：＿＿＿＿ ＿＿＿＿

（二）阅读

1. 读下面课文并选择合适的词语填空

新疆吐鲁番

我在中国游览过许多地方。如果有人问我："你最喜欢哪儿？"我会说："新疆的吐鲁番。"

夏日旅游，一般人喜欢到________的地方去，可我偏偏选择了________。那儿夏季白天的平均________在40℃左右。

吐鲁番是中国的葡萄王国，到处是________。远远望去，一片绿色。走近一看，才发现那一串串葡萄有绿色的、红色的、紫色的，还有黑色的，五颜六色，________极了。吐鲁番不只出产________，别的水果也多着呢。像甜甜的西瓜，红红的苹果，远近闻名的哈密瓜，你在那儿都可以看到。

我和朋友来到吐鲁番时正是夏天，________好客的吐鲁番人请我们吃了一次"水果宴"。每种水果只尝一点儿就吃饱了。等到上来烤全羊、手抓饭时，就再也吃不下了。饭后主人弹起冬不拉，唱起民歌，请我们一起________。歌声、琴声、笑声，那种欢乐的情景真比过节还________。

我还要告诉你，吐鲁番的沙子还能________呢。人们或躺或卧或跪或________，把沙子放在不舒服的部位上，一待就是三四个小时。这种方法叫"埋沙疗法"。________们说，这种"埋沙疗法"能________很多种病。

我在吐鲁番学会了一首民歌，叫《新疆好》。吐鲁番不就是这样一个好地方吗？如果有机会，我还要再去吐鲁番玩儿几天。

（凉快、好看、热情、热闹、葡萄、葡萄园、气温、专家、吐鲁番、坐、跳舞、治疗、治病）

2. 请说说"我"为什么最喜欢新疆吐鲁番。

3. 请谈谈学了这篇课文以后你知道了哪些信息。

（三）写作

以“……游记”为题，写一篇文章介绍你的一次旅游经历。

五 语法 Grammar

（一）时间补语 Temporal complement

1. 介词“于”的宾语可由表示时间序列点的词语充当，这种介宾短语可做时间补语。例如：

The object of the preposition “于” can be a word which refers to a point of time and this prepositional phrase can act as a temporal complement. For example:

（1）他出生于1976年。

（2）云冈石窟开凿于公元5世纪。

注意：这种补语限于书面语和较正式的口语。非正式的口语用“是 + 时点词语 + 动词 + 的”格式。例如：

Point for attention: This kind of complement appears only in written language or in formal circumstances, whereas the construction “是 + a word referring to a point of time + verb + 的” is used in informal spoken language. For example:

（3）他是1976年出生的。

（4）云冈石窟是公元5世纪开凿的。

2. 如果句中还有处所词语，时点词语要放在核心动词之前，处所词语可前可后，只是语体不同。例如：

If a locative phrase is also used in the sentence, the word referring to a point of time should be placed before the main verb, while the locative phrase can be put either before or after the main verb depending on different language style. For example:

（5）他是1976年在北京郊区出生的。（口语）

（6）他1976年出生于北京郊区。（书面语）

（二）“一＋量词＋名词”重叠 “一 + classifier + noun” reduplication

“一 + 量词 + 名词”这种短语可以重叠。其中，名词如果表示人或事物，重叠后表示逐指，强调依次进行某种活动。例如：

The phrase “一 + classifier + noun” can be reduplicated. If the noun refers to people or things, the reduplicated phrase indicates with emphasis that a certain activity is being conducted on one by one in proper order. For example:

（1）我们一个洞窟一个洞窟地参观。

（2）他一个房间一个房间地打扫。

注意：（1）这种短语重叠式只做状语。（2）这种短语中的名词所代表的人或事物在意念上是受事。（3）在语境明确的情况下，重叠式中的名词可省去，变成“一＋量词”的重叠式，即“一＋量词＋一＋量词”。例如：

Points for attention: (1) This phrase after reduplication can only act as an adverbial. (2) The people or things referred by the noun in the phrase are patients of the action notionally. (3) When the context is clear, the noun can be omitted when the phrase is reduplicated, so the phrase becomes “一 + classifier + 一 + classifier” after reduplication. For example:

（3）洞窟很多，我一个一个地参观。

（4）这么多房间，他一个一个地打扫。

Dì-jiǔ kè 第九课 研究研究

一 课文 Text

（艾米的朋友安娜在本市某大学学汉语。听说她最近心情不好，艾米去看她。）

艾　米：安娜，看你脸色不好，说话都没精神，怎么了？

安　娜：一连几夜失眠，饭也不想吃，心里不痛快。

艾　米：有什么心事，可以告诉老朋友吗？

安　娜：你瞧，我的房间正对着楼梯口，有的学生经过的时候说说笑笑、吵吵嚷嚷的，闹得人心烦，既学习不了，也睡不好觉。

艾　米：那你为什么不要求换个房间？

安　娜：我不是没提出这个要求。大前天我找到服务员，她说："这事儿我做不了主，得请示领导。"前天我又去问她，她说："你别着急，这事儿得研究研究哇！"昨天我在走廊上碰见她，她告诉我，科长出差还没回来，处长生病在家，其他负责人也不在，让我再等几天。上帝呀，再等，我非得精神病不可。

艾　米：他们办事儿怎么这么拖拉？

安　娜：我怎么也不明白，不就是换个房间吗？有什么值得研究的？

艾　米：这里的"研究"是考虑、商量和讨论的意思。有些事情他们不能马上决定就说"研究研究"，跟"研究中国文化"的"研究"不一样。

安　娜：这么点儿小事儿还用研究好几天吗？

艾　米：唉！谁知道怎么回事儿呢？

（有人敲门，安娜开门）

安　娜：是李科长，请进。您可是稀客。

李科长：你好，安娜。大前天，我急着出差开会，今天才回来，把你调房的事儿耽误了，真是对不起。我看340房间比较安静，你搬那儿去吧。

安　娜：谢谢，什么时候搬，还得研究研究吧？

李科长：这有什么可研究的？现在我就让服务员帮你搬过去。

二 生词 New words

1. 心情	（名）	xīnqíng	mood
2. 一连	（副）	yìlián	in a row, in succession
3. 失眠	（动）	shīmián	to lose sleep, to suffer from insomnia
4. 心里	（名）	xīnli	in the heart, at heart, in mind
5. 痛快	（形）	tòngkuai	delighted, joyful
6. 心事	（名）	xīnshì	worry, sth. weighing on one's mind
7. 楼梯	（名）	lóutī	stairs, staircase, stairway
8. 吵吵嚷嚷		chǎochǎorǎng-rǎng	to make a noise
吵嚷	（动）	chǎorǎng	to make a racket
吵	（动）	chǎo	to make a noise, to quarrel
嚷	（动）	rǎng	to shout, to yell, to make a noise
9. 心烦	（形）	xīnfán	upset, vexed, perturbed
烦	（形、动）	fán	annoying, irritated; to be annoyed, to be tired of

10. 请示	（动）	qǐngshì	to ask for instructions
11. 走廊	（名）	zǒuláng	corridor, passage
12. 碰见	（动）	pèngjiàn	to run into, to meet with
碰	（动）	pèng	to meet, to run into
13. 科长	（名）	kēzhǎng	section chief
14. 出差	（动）	chūchāi	to be on a business trip
15. 处长	（名）	chùzhǎng	division director
16. 其他	（代）	qítā	other, else
17. 负责人	（名）	fùzérén	person in charge
负责	（动）	fùzé	to be in charge of, to be responsible for
18. 非……不可		fēi…bù kě	must, have to
19. 精神病	（名）	jīngshénbìng	mental disease, psychosis
神经病	（名）	shénjīngbìng	neuropathy, nervous disease
20. 拖拉	（形）	tuōlā	slow, sluggish, dilatory
21. 调	（动）	tiáo	to change, to adjust

补充词汇　Supplementary words

1. 实践	（动）	shíjiàn	to put into practice, to carry out
2. 坚持	（动）	jiānchí	to insist on, to persist in, to stick to
3. 请求	（动、名）	qǐngqiú	to ask, to request; request
4. 原谅	（动）	yuánliàng	to excuse, to forgive, to pardon
5. 利用	（动）	lìyòng	to use, to make use of, to take advantage of
6. 活动	（名）	huódòng	activity, maneuver
7. 科学	（名、形）	kēxué	science; scientific
8. 集合	（动）	jíhé	to gather, to assemble
9. 友好	（形）	yǒuhǎo	friendly
10. 急救	（动）	jíjiù	to give first aid treatment
11. 相处	（动）	xiāngchǔ	to get along with (each other)
12. 提醒	（动）	tíxǐng	to remind, to call attention to
13. 危险	（形）	wēixiǎn	dangerous
14. 肺炎	（名）	fèiyán	pneumonia
15. 房东	（名）	fángdōng	landlord or landlady
16. 趣闻	（名）	qùwén	interesting news

17. 一衣带水		yìyīdàishuǐ	separated by a narrow strip of water, be continuous to each other
18. 文艺	（名）	wényì	literature and art
19. 幸亏	（副）	xìngkuī	luckily, fortunately
20. 广泛	（形）	guǎngfàn	extensive, broad, wide
21. 难以忘怀		nányǐ wànghuái	unforgettable, hard to forget
22. 集体	（名）	jítǐ	collective
23. 化解	（动）	huàjiě	to dissolve, to resolve
24. 陪伴	（动）	péibàn	to accompany, to keep sb. company
25. 担心	（动）	dānxīn	to worry, to feel anxious
26. 节约	（动）	jiéyuē	to save, to economize
27. 丰盛	（形）	fēngshèng	rich, sumptuous
28. 外人	（名）	wàirén	outsider, stranger
29. 薄	（形）	báo	thin, flimsy
30. 风雨交加		fēngyǔ jiāojiā	It's wet and windy, the wind howls and the rain pours
31. 拨打	（动）	bōdǎ	to dial, to call
32. 办理	（动）	bànlǐ	to deal with, to attend to
33. 手续	（名）	shǒuxù	procedures, formalities
34. 世世代代		shìshìdàidài	age after age, for generations
世代	（名）	shìdài	generations

专名　Proper nouns

1. 安娜	Ānnà	Anna, name of a person
2. 上帝	Shàngdì	God

二 课堂练习 Exercises

（一）语音

1. 辨音辨调

qǐnshì	寝室	xìngmíng	姓名	shíjiàn	实践
qǐngshì	请示	xìngmìng	性命	shíxiàn	实现

jiānchí	坚持	qǐqiú	企求	yuánliàng	原谅
jiāngchí	僵持	qǐngqiú	请求	yuánliào	原料

2. 四音节声调

利用机会	坚持锻炼	纪念活动	信息科学
利用经验	坚持训练	庆祝活动	自然科学
利用知识	坚持工作	破坏活动	历史科学
利用关系	坚持创作	秘密活动	社会科学

3. 语调

（1）我怎么也不明白，不就是换个房间吗？有什么值得研究的？

（2）我怎么也不明白，不就是调个房间吗？有什么值得请示的？

（3）我怎么也不明白，不就是写错个字吗？有什么值得奇怪的？

（4）我怎么也不明白，不就是说错个词吗？有什么值得道歉的？

（二）词语

1. 连线并朗读

请示	实践
坚持	时间
集合	领导
语言	痛快
友好	劳动
体育	出差
心里	相处
办事儿	活动
去南方	科学
学习	同意
请求	电话
急救	拖拉

2. 从本课生词表中选择合适的词语填空

（1）他________不好的时候总喜欢一个人听歌。

（2）昨天夜里我________了，今天有点儿头疼。

（3）这件事儿你能做主吗？要不要________领导？

（4）今天跟你们一起聊天儿，聊得真________！

（5）你们别________了，我心里________着呢。

（6）老张去年是科长，今年升________了。

（7）你有什么________？能告诉我吗？

（8）我在街上________了一个老朋友。

（9）谁是这儿的________？

（10）上星期你去哪儿________了？

（11）如果这个问题解决了，________问题就好办了。

（12）请你________王才，明天下午两点在学校西门________。

（13）这儿________！你们别过来。

（14）请你________，我把时间记错了。

（15）你的意见是错误的，不要________了。

（16）我想________这次旅行的机会多了解了解中国的民俗。

（17）大夫说我得了________________________。

（18）我的________是中国人。

（19）他说的________真有意思。

（20）汉语节目表演是语言________活动。

（21）中国和日本是________________的邻居。

（22）艾米从小爱好________，什么唱歌、跳舞、弹琴她都喜欢。

（23）这个病人________送得及时。

（24）他的爱好非常________。

（25）这是我一生中________________的事。

（三）句型

替换

（1）我不是没提出这个要求。

告诉他

提醒他

通知他

帮助他

原谅他

坚持这个意见

利用这个机会

使用这个方法

给他发邀请信

给他调房

（2）他不是不知道集合时间。

知道集合地点

知道这很危险

喜欢参加语言实践活动

喜欢体育锻炼

喜欢参加集体活动

明白你的意思

同意你的意见

答应你的请求

相信科学

爱好文艺

（3）没有人不认识他。

喜欢

相信

尊敬

佩服

赞扬

反对

重视

原谅

答应

请示

(4) 我非得精神病不可。

你	得感冒
你	去医院
你	打针
你	迟到
他	调房
他	改时间
他	去西安
他	买汽车
他们	参加比赛
他们	使用这个方法

(5) 闹得人心烦，既学习不了，也睡不好觉。

吃不下饭	睡不好觉
学习不了	休息不了
工作不了	休息不了
学习不了	工作不了
不能学习	不能休息
不能学习	不能工作

四 家庭作业 Homework

（一）词语

1. 用下列生词至少组成两个短语

（1）碰见：________ ________　（2）化解：________ ________

（3）提醒：________ ________　（4）原谅：________ ________

（5）坚持：________ ________　（6）利用：________ ________

（7）集合：________ ________　（8）实践：________ ________

（9）活动：________ ________　（10）请求：________ ________

（11）陪伴：________ ________　（12）危险：________ ________

2. 用括号里的结构改写句子

（1）我提醒过他，可他还是忘了。　（不是没……）

（2）我确实给他打电话了，他家没有人。　（不是没……）

（3）我很想参加书法学习班，只是没有时间。　（不是不……）

（4）我同意你的意见，只是不同意你的态度。　（不是不……）

（5）艾米在速成学院很有名，大家都认识她。　（没……不……）

（6）那个孩子长得非常可爱，大家都很喜欢他。　（没……不……）

（7）这儿离火车站很远，我们只能坐出租车去。　（非……不可）

（8）你感冒了，必须打针吃药。　（非……不可）

（二）阅读

我的中国房东

我的房东是两位中国老人，他们的年纪跟我的爷爷奶奶差不多，所以我称呼他们爷爷和奶奶。

第一次到北京留学，我很想跟中国人住在一起，可是又有点儿担心，我怕因为生活习惯不同而发生矛盾。跟房东第一次见面以后，我的担心就化解了。那天下午，一个朋友带我来到现在的新家。我对房子很满意，谈好价钱以后，爷爷对我说："孩子，从今天开始，我们就像一家人一样，你不要客气，有什么困难和要求就告诉我们。家里所有的东西都随便用，不要重新买。你是个学生，一定要节约用钱才好。"几句话说得我心里暖暖的，他们就像我的亲爷爷奶奶一样。

每到周末，奶奶都为他们的儿女还有孙子准备丰盛的饭菜，一家人吃团圆饭。他们也邀请我参加聚会，刚开始我怕给他们增添麻烦，不好意思参加。后来，随着关系越来越熟，我也不把自己当外人了，我主动帮奶奶做饭，有时还做一两个日本小菜。奶奶做的菜非常好吃，特别是她包的饺子，皮薄馅儿多，我从来没吃过那么好吃的饺子。我跟他们一边吃饭一边谈话。他们谈的话题非常广泛，有国内外发生的大事，也有一些生活趣闻。因为我是外国人，为了让我听懂，他们说得比平时慢，有时候还给我解释。我也给他们介绍我的老师、我的同学、我学过的课文。跟他们一起谈话，我的汉语水平提高得很快。

有一次，我新买的电动车丢了，心里很难过，回家以后跟奶奶说了。第二天放学回到家，爷爷把一辆旧电动车推到我面前，说："孩子，住在北京，没有电动车不方便。你不要再买新的了。这辆车看起来旧，可是很好骑。我把它擦洗了一下，明天你就骑着它去上学吧。对了，这是旧车，你不用担心被人偷了。"为了擦洗这辆电动车，爷爷花了整整一个下午的时间。看着爷爷给我的电动车，我真不知道说什么才好。

最令我难以忘怀的是一个风雨交加的晚上，我咳嗽，发高烧，呼吸困难。爷爷奶奶听见我咳嗽，赶快跑过来。爷爷马上拨打120急救电话，把我送到医院。爷爷为我排队挂号、交费、取药、办理住院手续，奶奶一直陪伴在我身边。医生说我得的是肺炎，幸亏送得及时。那天，爷爷奶奶回到家已经是后半夜了。据说他们的衣服都湿了，里边是汗水，外边是雨水。

还有一个月我就毕业了。回到日本以后，我要把我在中国留学的经历告诉我的家人和朋友。我要告诉他们，中国和日本是一衣带水的好邻居，两国人民一定能够世世代代地友好相处。

读后回答

(1) 课文中的“我”是哪国人?

(2) 课文中写了“我”跟房东一起生活的哪几件事儿?

(3) 第一次到北京留学,“我”担心什么?这担心是怎么化解的?

(4) 房东邀请“我”参加聚会,“我”为什么不想参加?后来又有什么变化?

(5)“我”的电动车丢了以后,发生了什么事情?

(6) 最令“我”难以忘怀的是什么事情?

(7)“我”回国以后要做什么?

五 语法 Grammar

(一) 二次否定 Double negations

二次否定可以表示肯定、持中等意思。表示肯定的,例如:

A double negations can be used to express affirmation, moderation and so on. The following sentences indicate affirmation:

(1) 艾米:那你为什么不要求换个房间?

安娜:我不是没提出这个要求。

(2) A:他可能不知道。

B:我不相信他不知道。

表示持中的,例如:

The following sentences indicate moderation:

(3) 他没有说这样做不对。

(4) 我没说不同意。

（二）强调的表达法（4） The way to express emphasis (4)

二次否定表示肯定意义时，肯定的程度是有所不同的，其一是强式肯定。这种强式肯定也是表示强调的一种表达方法。例如：

When a double negations is used to indicate affirmation, the degree of affirmation may vary. A strong affirmation indicated by double negations is one of the ways to express emphasis. For example:

（1）他在我们学校很有名，没有人不认识他。

（2）再等，我非得精神病不可。

Dì-shí kè
第十课 点歌送真情

一 课文 Text

如今，许多出租车司机都有边开车边听广播的习惯，王师傅就是其中一位。他每天不仅听小说、听音乐，还通过广播了解实时路况和国内外发生的大事小情。

在广播电台里给朋友点播一首歌，是王师傅和他的司机朋友们最喜爱做的事情。他们经常为圈子里的人点歌，有人过生日，就点一首《祝你生日快乐》，祝福他天天开心，事事顺利；有人结婚，就点一首《最浪漫的事》，祝福新郎新娘美满幸福，白头到老。每一支歌曲里，都充满了他们的友谊、他们的快乐。

“打开点歌台，聆听真情的声音。各位好！欢迎收听我们的节目。我非常喜欢我们栏目的这句宣传语，因为真情是我们生活的必需品，而点歌台真诚地希望能够成为大家无话不说的音乐好伙伴……”王师傅跟往常一样听着电台里传来的广播。今天他拉了几单大活儿，心情非常好，他想找个地方吃点儿东西。刚停好车，突然他听见广播里传来主持人的声音：“136手机尾号2058的王师傅，您在收听我们的节目吗？您的女儿有话要对您说。”王师傅像是被电到了一样，愣了。

“爸爸，今天我收到了大学录取通知书！打开通知书那一刻，我的眼泪止不住地流下来。爸爸，谢谢您！是您的辛劳支撑了这个家，让我能够无忧无虑地专心学习。爸爸，每天您早出晚归，和您一起吃晚饭的次数太少太少了。今天我和妈妈一起做了晚饭，都是您爱吃的。您今天能不能早点儿回家？我和妈妈在家等着您。”

“王师傅，您听到了吗？首先我们栏目组全体工作人员祝贺您的女儿考上了理想的大学，我们也为您有这么优秀的女儿感到高兴。王师傅，如果可能的话，就早点儿回家吧。路上注意安全。”

听到这里，王师傅已经热泪盈眶。

“爸爸，我为您、为妈妈，也为我自己点了一首歌，是我小时候您和妈妈经常唱给我听的《宝贝》。爸爸，女儿永远都是您的宝贝。”

二 生词 New words

1. 点歌		diǎn gē	to request a song for broadcasting or televising
2. 真情	（名）	zhēnqíng	genuine feelings, true feelings
3. 如今	（名）	rújīn	nowadays, now, at present
4. 其中	（名）	qízhōng	among, in, inside
5. 通过	（介）	tōngguò	by means of, by way of
6. 实时	（副）	shíshí	in actual time, in real time
7. 路况	（名）	lùkuàng	road conditions, traffic
8. 电台	（名）	diàntái	radio station
9. 点播	（动）	diǎnbō	(of a listener) to ask the radio station to broadcast one's requested item
播	（动）	bō	to broadcast
10. 喜爱	（动）	xǐ'ài	to like, to be fond of
11. 圈子	（名）	quānzi	circle, group
12. 祝福	（动）	zhùfú	to bless, to wish happiness to
13. 新郎	（名）	xīnláng	bridegroom
14. 新娘	（名）	xīnniáng	bride
15. 美满	（形）	měimǎn	happy, perfectly satisfactory
16. 聆听	（动）	língtīng	to listen to (respectfully)
17. 收听	（动）	shōutīng	to listen in
18. 栏目	（名）	lánmù	the heading or title of column (in a newspaper, magazine, TV, etc.)
19. 宣传语	（名）	xuānchuányǔ	conduct propaganda
宣传	（动）	xuānchuán	to propagate, to publicize
20. 必需品	（名）	bìxūpǐn	necessaries, necessities
必需	（动）	bìxū	to be necessary, to be essential

21. 真诚	（形）	zhēnchéng	sincere, true, honest
22. 无话不说		wúhuà-bùshuō	to chat with sb. without reserve
23. 往常	（名）	wǎngcháng	habitually in the past
24. 传	（动）	chuán	to spread
25. 拉活儿	（动）	lāhuór	(of taixs, minibuses) to take on passengers
26. 单	（量）	dān	a measure word for business for signing contracts
27. 尾号	（名）	wěihào	end of the number (of a mobile phone, telephone, etc.)
28. 录取	（动）	lùqǔ	to enroll, to recruit
29. 辛劳	（形）	xīnláo	toilsome, laborious, tired
30. 支撑	（动）	zhīchēng	to prop up, to sustain, to support
31. 无忧无虑		wúyōu-wúlǜ	to be free from care, without sorrow and anxiety
32. 早出晚归		zǎochū-wǎnguī	to go out early and come back at dusk
归		guī	to return, to go back to
33. 全体	（名）	quántǐ	all, entire, whole
34. 热泪盈眶		rèlèi yíng kuàng	one's eyes run over with tears
35. 宝贝	（名）	bǎobei	baby, treasure

补充词汇 Supplementary words

1. 感情	（名）	gǎnqíng	feeling, emotion, sentiment
2. 为人	（名）	wéirén	behavior, conduct
3. 干涉	（动）	gānshè	to interfere, to intervene
4. 赚	（动）	zhuàn	to make a profit, to earn
5. 撞	（动）	zhuàng	to collide, to bump into, to bump against
6. 热烈	（形）	rèliè	warm, enthusiastic
7. 坦率	（形）	tǎnshuài	frank, straightforward
8. 吻	（动）	wěn	to kiss
9. 收获	（名）	shōuhuò	gains, results
10. 搞	（动）	gǎo	to do, to carry on
11. 宫殿	（名）	gōngdiàn	palace

12. 万一	（连）	wànyī	just in case, if by any chance
13. 利息	（名）	lìxī	interest
14. 税	（名）	shuì	tax
15. 补	（动）	bǔ	to make up for, to fill up
16. 光	（形）	guāng	used up, with nothing left
17. 棒	（形）	bàng	good, fine, excellent
18. 富	（形）	fù	rich
19. 穷	（形）	qióng	poor
20. 躲	（动）	duǒ	to hide, to avoid
21. 毕竟	（副）	bìjìng	after all, all in all
22. 孙子	（名）	sūnzi	grandson
23. 做法	（名）	zuòfa	way of doing, method of work
24. 发愁	（动）	fāchóu	to worry, to be anxious
25. 澳元	（名）	àoyuán	Australian dollar

专名　Proper nouns

1. 卢京生	Lú Jīngshēng	name of a person
2. 希尔顿饭店	Xī'ěrdùn Fàndiàn	Hilton Hotel

二　课堂练习 Exercises

（一）语音

1. 辨音辨调

zhùfú	祝福	yùnhé	运河	zhēnqíng	真情
zhìfú	制服	rènhé	任何	shēnqíng	深情
zhēnchéng	真诚	lùqǔ	录取	yǒuhǎo	友好
zhēngchéng	征程	rù jú	入局	yàohǎo	要好

2. 四音节声调

喜爱京剧	感情丰富	点播歌曲	全体老师
喜爱歌剧	感情深厚	点播音乐	全体医生
喜爱音乐	感情不错	点播京剧	全体职员
喜爱雕塑	感情浪漫	点播故事	全体作家

（二）词语

1. 连线并朗读

传	美满
受到	歌曲
生活	栏目
点播	晚归
实时	喜爱
收听	坦率
早出	钱
为人	同学
干涉	车
全体	新闻
赚	吻
撞	别人
热烈的	礼物

2. 从本课生词表中选择合适的词语填空

（1）彼得特别________小动物，他常常去动物园玩儿。

（2）我非常珍惜我们的________。

（3）我________地希望爸爸妈妈健康长寿。

（4）这个城市的交通________给我留下了很深的印象。

（5）来中国后他很快就认识了很多朋友，并且有了新的生活和工作________。

(6) 今天是我的生日，我的男朋友在电台为我________了一首歌曲。

(7) 这里的人民过着幸福________的生活。

(8) 他同时收到了两所大学的________通知书。

(9) 中国有句老话：一分________，一分收获。

(10) 这件事情最重要，一定要________好。

(11) 那位老演员的表演________丰富，给我留下了很深的印象。

(12) 他________地说出自己的看法。

(13) 请不要________别人的感情生活。

(14) 故宫里的每个________都有自己的故事。

(15) ________明天下雨，我们还去参观吗？

(16) 30多年后再次见面，让两位老人______________。

(17) 在中国，让孩子有一个______________的童年就是父母的幸福。

(18) 只有下大本钱（běnqián，capital），才能________更多的钱。

(19) 他们国家规定，银行存钱产生的利息不上________。

(20) 现在银行的________减少了。

(21) 大内昨天没做作业，她今天________上了。

(22) 我的钱花________了，得去银行取钱了。

(23) 他英语说得真________！

(24) 在这个城市，一些人很________，有楼房和汽车；一些人很________，连饭也吃不饱。

3. 用“搞”填空，并体会不同的意思

(1) 今天下午老师们________卫生，打扫宿舍和办公室。

(2) 这个月赵工程师________了三项设计。

(3) 我们要把经济工作________上去。

(4) 这个问题必须________清楚。

(5) 那个孩子把衣服________得很脏。

(6) 他们这个星期特别忙，每天都________得很晚才回家。

(7) 你是不是________错了？这不是我说的。

（三）功能会话：听后模仿

1. 推测

（1）A：他怎么没告诉我？
　　B：他会告诉你的。

（2）A：他能恢复健康吗？
　　B：他会恢复健康的。

（3）A：他会参加比赛吗？
　　B：他身体不太好，不会参加的。

（4）A：他会同意这么做吗？
　　B：不会的。

2. 确认

（1）A：他打扫得干干净净。
　　B：是挺干净。

（2）A：她今天穿得挺漂亮。
　　B：是挺漂亮。

3. 询问人或物的方位或处所（2）

（1）A：你把自行车放在哪儿了？
　　B：我把自行车放在宿舍门口了。

（2）A：你把电视搬到哪儿去了？
　　B：我把电视搬到山本宿舍去了。

4. 询问原因或目的（2）

（1）A：你怎么没把孩子带来？
　　B：我把他送到幼儿园去了。

（2）A：你怎么把自行车卖了？
　　B：我想买辆新的。

5. 征求意见

（1）A：我把姑娘的照片带来了，你看看怎么样？

　　B：是挺漂亮。

（2）A：我把小伙子的照片带来了，你看看怎么样？

　　B：是挺精神。

6. 追问

（1）A：这儿的冬天冷得很。

　　B：到底有多冷呢？

　　A：最低气温零下20度。

（2）A：我们学校离市中心很远。

　　B：到底有多远呢？

　　A：20公里左右。

四 家庭作业 Homework

（一）词语

1. 用下列生词至少组成两个短语

（1）传：________ ________　　（2）聆听：________ ________

（3）宣传：________ ________　　（4）搞：________ ________

（5）躲：________ ________　　（6）补：________ ________

（7）撞：________ ________　　（8）赚：________ ________

（9）喜爱：________ ________　　（10）干涉：________ ________

（11）坦率：________ ________　　（12）圈子：________ ________

2. 用"毕竟"完成句子

（1）他们经过努力，最后______________了。（成功）

(2) 那位老大爷虽然身体很好，可是他_____________了。(70岁)

(3) 艾米看了一些有关中国文化的书，可是理解还不够深，因为她___________________。(外国人)

(4) 学语言跟学文学_________________。(不一样)

(5) 你们现在虽然离了婚，可是她以前_______________，能帮忙就帮忙吧。(妻子)

(6) 那些学生___________________(年轻)，社会经验还不丰富。

(二) 阅读

卢京生和玛丽

(方云天的老同学卢京生从澳大利亚回国看望朋友。一天，卢京生来看望方云天，方云天问："听说你早就有了女朋友，怎么到现在还不结婚？"卢京生笑着摇摇头，讲了他和女友玛丽的故事。)

我和玛丽是在上学期间认识的。我们俩感情一直不错，但是，只要我一提结婚，她的回答就是"NO"。我是独生子(dúshēngzǐ，only son)，我妈每个月都打电话催我结婚，她老人家急着抱孙子。有一天，我把我妈的想法告诉了玛丽，她听了笑着说："你妈、孩子，这些和我们的爱有什么关系？你们中国人的爱就是水分(shuǐfèn，surplus exaggeration)多！"

玛丽为人坦率热情，可是有些做法实在让我很难接受。

有一次，她爸爸来看她，她却躲在屋里不见。我说："虽然他很早就和你妈妈离了婚，没有给你多少父爱，可他毕竟是你的父亲哪！"她一听就火了："别把我当成孩子！咱们俩谁也别干涉对方的私事！"

看起来她好像不愿干涉别人的事，可有时不是那么回事儿。去年我报税时，差点儿忘报银行利息。她知道后，一定要帮我上税，弄得我很不好意思。

她总笑话我喜欢存钱，说："万一明天撞了车，你的钱留给谁？不要学怎样存钱，要学怎样赚钱，懂不懂？"

去年冬天，我们去几个城市旅游了一圈儿，钱几乎花光了。她发了愁："怎么办呢？明天我们只能吃干面包了。"

第二天，我从银行里取出了仅有的500澳元。玛丽见我又有钱了，她给我一个热烈的吻，拉起我就走："听说希尔顿饭店像座宫殿。走，咱们去住一夜，过过富人的生活。"

"可我们是穷人。"

"不，今天还不是！"

那一夜，她的富人生活把这点儿钱花得干干净净。

第二天，我们走出"宫殿"的时候，真的变成了穷人，她笑着握住我的手，大声说："太棒了！"没想到，我教她的这句中国话，她用在这儿了！

1. 下面哪些是玛丽的想法和做法？（在句子后面括号内打"✓"或"×"）

(1) 结婚是为了生孩子。（ ）

(2) 结婚只是为了爱情。（ ）

(3) 不见自己的父亲。（ ）

(4) 应该见自己的父亲。（ ）

(5) 补交银行利息产生的税。（ ）

(6) 喜欢存钱。（ ）

(7) 赚钱比存钱重要。（ ）

(8) 有钱就把它花光。（ ）

2. 卢京生和玛丽认识了很长时间，为什么到现在还不结婚？

3. 你对不同国家的人结婚有什么看法？

（三）写作

根据阅读课文的内容或者你了解的情况，以"我看跨国婚姻"为题，写一篇文章说明你的观点。

五 语法 Grammar

补语的分类 Types of complements

在汉语里，补语主要有以下几种：

In Chinese, there are several kinds of complements:

1. 结果补语，又可细分为：

Resultative complement, which can be subdivided into:

① 强调过程发展阶段的。例如：

Some of resultative complements emphasize the stage in the course of development. For example:

（1）他唱起来了。（始发性的）

（2）这么早，他们就开始干上活儿了。（始发性的）

（3）这孩子个儿又长高了。（中止性的）

（4）他们班学到第10课了，我们班才学到第6课。（中止性的）

（5）这个工作还得干下去。（继续性的）

（6）请你接着念下去！（继续性的）

（7）这篇文章，他翻译完了。（终结性的）

（8）他没有住上新房呢。（终结性的）

② 不强调过程发展阶段，只强调状态变化的。例如：

Some of resultative complements do not emphasize the stage in the course of development, but only stress the change of state. For example:

（9）睡了两天两夜之后，老人终于醒过来了。

（10）他的衣服还在外面，我的衣服收起来了。

2. 趋向补语，例如：

Directional complement, for example:

（1）他把照相机拿来了。（一般动词 + 来/去）

（2）他给爸爸寄去了一封信。（一般动词 + 来/去）

（3）他回家去了。（“上”类动词 + 来/去）

（4）他进屋去了。（“上”类动词＋来/去）

（5）他买回了一些水果。（一般动词＋“上”类动词）

（6）他搬进了一张桌子。（一般动词＋“上”类动词）

（7）他家搬到新楼去了。（一般动词＋“上”类动词＋来/去）

（8）他拿起照相机来给我照了一张相。（一般动词＋“上”类动词＋来/去）

3. 可能补语，例如：

Potential complement, for example:

（1）作业太多，我一个小时做不完。（得/不＋一般动词/形容词）

（2）下雨了，进不了城了。（得/不＋动词“了”）

（3）他的腿摔坏了，站不起来了。（得/不＋趋向动词）

（4）这个人批评不得。（得/不得）

4. 状态补语，例如：

State complement, for example:

（1）他唱得比较好。（评议性的）

（2）他说得很流利。（评议性的）

（3）他急得心里直冒火。（描写性的）

（4）急得他心里直冒火。（描写性的）

5. 程度补语，例如：

Degree complement, for example:

（1）他的病好多了。（不带“得”）

（2）我的肚子疼极了。（不带“得”）

（3）他疼得不得了。（带“得”）

（4）丝绸贵得要命。（带“得”）

6. 数量补语，例如：

Quantitive complement, for example:

（1）我看一下。（动量）

（2）他去过两次。（动量）

（3）我休息一会儿。（时量）

（4）他大学毕业两年了。（时量）

（5）今年的学生比去年增加了一倍。（物量）

（6）我的笔少了一支。（物量）

7. 处所补语，由介词“于”及其宾语组成的介宾短语充当。例如：

Locative complement, which is composed of the preposition “于” and its object. For example:

（1）茶最早产于中国。

（2）他毕业于北京大学。

8. 时间补语。这里的“时间”指时间序列点。这种补语由介词“于”及其宾语组成的介宾短语充当。例如：

Temporal complement. Here “time” refers to a point of time. This type of complement is composed of the preposition “于” and its object. For example:

（1）他生于1970年。

（2）这本小说写于1980年。

Glossary
词汇总表

A			
安排	（动）	ānpái	1
安全带	（名）	ānquándài	2
澳元	（名）	àoyuán	10
AA 制	（名）	AA zhì	1
B			
百科全书		bǎikē quánshū	6
办理	（动）	bànlǐ	9
棒	（形）	bàng	10
包子	（名）	bāozi	1
薄	（形）	báo	9
宝贝	（名）	bǎobei	10
宝库	（名）	bǎokù	8
保护	（动）	bǎohù	8
笔	（量）	bǐ	6
必需	（动）	bìxū	10
必需品	（名）	bìxūpǐn	10
毕竟	（副）	bìjìng	10
碧螺春	（名）	bìluóchūn	7
扁	（形）	biǎn	1
变迁	（动）	biànqiān	6
拨打	（动）	bōdǎ	9
波浪	（名）	bōlàng	6
播	（动）	bō	10
不愧	（副）	búkuì	5
不是……而是……		bú shì… ér shì…	3
补	（动）	bǔ	10
补充	（动）	bǔchōng	7
不仅	（连）	bùjǐn	3
不同	（形）	bùtóng	1
部	（量）	bù	6
部位	（名）	bùwèi	8
C			
采	（动）	cǎi	3
彩色	（名）	cǎisè	4
残缺	（动）	cánquē	8
茶馆儿	（名）	cháguǎnr	7
茶园	（名）	cháyuán	7
产	（动）	chǎn	4
场所	（名）	chǎngsuǒ	7
超过	（动）	chāoguò	7
朝	（介）	cháo	2
朝		cháo	3
朝代	（名）	cháodài	3
吵	（动）	chǎo	9
吵吵嚷嚷		chǎochǎorǎng-rǎng	9
吵嚷	（动）	chǎorǎng	9
车窗	（名）	chēchuāng	2
沉	（动）	chén	7
称	（动）	chēng	6
称呼	（动）	chēnghu	5
称赞	（动）	chēngzàn	8
称作	（动）	chēngzuò	6
成立	（动）	chénglì	8
出差	（动）	chūchāi	9

出口	（动）	chūkǒu	7
出现	（动）	chūxiàn	8
处长	（名）	chùzhǎng	9
传	（动）	chuán	10
串	（量）	chuàn	8
创作	（动）	chuàngzuò	8
从……起		cóng…qǐ	6
粗	（形）	cū	2
粗重	（形）	cūzhòng	2
醋	（名）	cù	1
D			
达到	（动）	dádào	5
打搅	（动）	dǎjiǎo	4
打扰	（动）	dǎrǎo	4
大使	（名）	dàshǐ	2
大使馆	（名）	dàshǐguǎn	2
待	（动）	dāi	8
担心	（动）	dānxīn	9
单	（量）	dān	10
淡	（形）	dàn	1
当天	（名）	dàngtiān	4
道德	（名）	dàodé	5
得名	（动）	démíng	6
地区	（名）	dìqū	1
点播	（动）	diǎnbō	10
点歌		diǎn gē	10
电台	（名）	diàntái	10
雕塑	（名）	diāosù	8
洞	（名）	dòng	8
洞窟	（名）	dòngkū	8
都		dū	3
毒	（名）	dú	7
对……来说		duì…lái shuō	3
朵	（量）	duǒ	4
躲	（动）	duǒ	10
F			
发愁	（动）	fāchóu	10
法学	（名）	fǎxué	7
烦	（形、动）	fán	9
反对	（动）	fǎnduì	5
反映	（动）	fǎnyìng	5
方	（形）	fāng	1
房东	（名）	fángdōng	9
非……不可		fēi…bù kě	9
肺炎	（名）	fèiyán	9
费用	（名）	fèiyong	3
分	（动）	fēn	4
分不开		fēn bu kāi	4
分开	（动）	fēnkāi	4
分配	（动）	fēnpèi	3
份	（量）	fèn	1
丰富	（形）	fēngfù	6
丰盛	（形）	fēngshèng	9
风景	（名）	fēngjǐng	3
风俗	（名）	fēngsú	6
风雨交加		fēngyǔ jiāojiā	9
佛	（名）	fó	8
佛像	（名）	fóxiàng	8
扶	（动）	fú	4
浮	（动）	fú	7
负责	（动）	fùzé	9
负责人	（名）	fùzérén	9
复		fù	4
复活	（动）	fùhuó	4
富	（形）	fù	10
G			
改造	（动）	gǎizào	6

干	（形）	gān	1
干涉	（动）	gānshè	10
赶紧	（副）	gǎnjǐn	5
赶快	（副）	gǎnkuài	2
感情	（名）	gǎnqíng	10
感兴趣		gǎn xìngqù	6
高峰	（名）	gāofēng	2
高尚	（形）	gāoshàng	5
搞	（动）	gǎo	10
告辞	（动）	gàocí	4
个儿	（名）	gèr	3
各种各样		gèzhǒng-gèyàng	1
根	（量）	gēn	1
根本	（副）	gēnběn	2
公公	（名）	gōnggong	5
公元	（名）	gōngyuán	8
功能	（名）	gōngnéng	7
宫殿	（名）	gōngdiàn	10
古都	（名）	gǔdū	3
官	（名）	guān	5
光	（形）	guāng	10
广泛	（形）	guǎngfàn	9
归		guī	10
跪	（动）	guì	8
国外	（名）	guówài	3
果然	（副）	guǒrán	1

H

哈密瓜	（名）	hāmìguā	8
海员	（名）	hǎiyuán	4
害怕	（动）	hàipà	4
行业	（名）	hángyè	6
和气	（形）	héqi	2
黑	（形）	hēi	2
后悔	（动）	hòuhuǐ	5
呼	（动）	hū	6
呼吸	（动）	hūxī	6
胡同	（名）	hútòng	6
壶	（名）	hú	7
户	（量）	hù	4
花茶	（名）	huāchá	7
化解	（动）	huàjiě	9
化学	（名）	huàxué	8
欢乐	（形）	huānlè	8
缓和	（形）	huǎnhé	5
灰	（形）	huī	6
灰色	（名）	huīsè	6
回忆	（动）	huíyì	3
馄饨	（名）	húntun	1
活动	（名）	huódòng	9

J

急救	（动）	jíjiù	9
集合	（动）	jíhé	9
集体	（名）	jítǐ	9
计划	（动、名）	jìhuà	1
记录	（动）	jìlù	6
技术	（名）	jìshù	8
系	（动）	jì	2
继续	（动）	jìxù	5
加	（动）	jiā	6
佳	（形）	jiā	1
家乡	（名）	jiāxiāng	3
价钱	（名）	jiàqian	4
嫁	（动）	jià	1
坚持	（动）	jiānchí	9
拣	（动）	jiǎn	3

简直	（副）	jiǎnzhí	7
江	（名）	jiāng	3
讲究	（动）	jiǎngjiu	5
酱油	（名）	jiàngyóu	1
交流	（动）	jiāoliú	7
脚	（名）	jiǎo	4
教育	（动、名）	jiàoyù	4
街道	（名）	jiēdào	6
节约	（动）	jiéyuē	9
洁白	（形）	jiébái	3
解毒	（动）	jiědú	7
解围	（动）	jiěwéi	5
介意	（动）	jièyì	2
仅	（副）	jǐn	3
进修	（动）	jìnxiū	1
经验	（名）	jīngyàn	4
精神病	（名）	jīngshénbìng	9
精致	（形）	jīngzhì	1
井	（名）	jǐng	6
敬	（动）	jìng	7
究竟	（副）	jiūjìng	3
鞠躬	（动）	jūgōng	2
俱	（副）	jù	1
据说	（动）	jùshuō	5
聚会	（动）	jùhuì	7
K			
开凿	（动）	kāizáo	8
科学	（名、形）	kēxué	9
科长	（名）	kēzhǎng	9
口味	（名）	kǒuwèi	1
夸张	（形）	kuāzhāng	6
快餐	（名）	kuàicān	1
矿泉水	（名）	kuàngquán-shuǐ	7

L			
拉活儿	（动）	lāhuór	10
栏目	（名）	lánmù	10
劳动	（动、名）	láodòng	4
老百姓	（名）	lǎobǎixìng	7
类	（名、量）	lèi	1
愣	（动）	lèng	2
礼貌	（形、名）	lǐmào	2
里弄	（名）	lǐlòng	6
理	（动）	lǐ	2
利息	（名）	lìxī	10
利用	（动）	lìyòng	9
例如	（动）	lìrú	5
连声	（副）	liánshēng	4
联系	（动）	liánxì	2
了不起	（形）	liǎobuqǐ	5
灵感	（名）	línggǎn	8
聆听	（动）	língtīng	10
留念	（动）	liúniàn	8
流	（动）	liú	3
龙井	（名）	lóngjǐng	7
楼梯	（名）	lóutī	9
录取	（动）	lùqǔ	10
路况	（名）	lùkuàng	10
旅伴	（名）	lǚbàn	8
乱	（形）	luàn	5
M			
埋	（动）	mái	8
买单	（动）	mǎidān	1
满月	（动）	mǎnyuè	5
毛	（名）	máo	6
毛峰	（名）	máofēng	7
冒火	（动）	màohuǒ	2

眉毛	（名）	méimao	3
美满	（形）	měimǎn	10
美术	（名）	měishù	8
猛然	（副）	měngrán	2
秘密	（名）	mìmì	1
面	（名）	miàn	7
苗条	（形）	miáotiao	3
名称	（名）	míngchēng	6
命名	（动）	mìngmíng	6
茉莉花	（名）	mòlìhuā	7
茉莉花茶	（名）	mòlìhuāchá	7
牧民	（名）	mùmín	7
		N	
奶茶	（名）	nǎichá	7
男声	（名）	nánshēng	2
难得	（形）	nándé	5
难以忘怀		nányǐ wàng-huái	9
牛毛	（名）	niúmáo	6
浓	（形）	nóng	6
浓厚	（形）	nónghòu	6
女声	（名）	nǚshēng	2
		P	
拍摄	（动）	pāishè	8
拍照	（动）	pāizhào	8
排	（动、名）	pái	1
排队	（动）	páiduì	1
排列	（动）	páiliè	6
盼	（动）	pàn	5
盼望	（动）	pànwàng	5
陪伴	（动）	péibàn	9
佩服	（动）	pèifu	2
碰	（动）	pèng	9
碰见	（动）	pèngjiàn	9
皮	（名）	pí	3
皮肤	（名）	pífū	3
脾气	（名）	píqi	4
偏	（副）	piān	8
偏偏	（副）	piānpiān	8
平静	（形）	píngjìng	2
平均	（动）	píngjūn	8
平台	（名）	píngtái	2
婆婆	（名）	pópo	5
破坏	（动）	pòhuài	8
		Q	
其次	（代）	qícì	7
其他	（代）	qítā	9
其中	（名）	qízhōng	10
奇特	（形）	qítè	6
启发	（动）	qǐfā	8
起名儿	（动）	qǐmíngr	5
洽谈	（动）	qiàtán	7
迁居	（动）	qiānjū	3
浅	（形）	qiǎn	2
亲切	（形）	qīnqiè	2
亲手	（副）	qīnshǒu	4
亲眼	（副）	qīnyǎn	8
亲自	（副）	qīnzì	6
琴	（名）	qín	8
清	（形）	qīng	3
情景	（名）	qíngjǐng	8
请求	（动、名）	qǐngqiú	9
请示	（动）	qǐngshì	9
穷	（形）	qióng	10
区别	（名）	qūbié	1
曲艺	（名）	qǔyì	7
趣闻	（名）	qùwén	9

圈子	（名）	quānzi	10
全面	（形）	quánmiàn	5
全体	（名）	quántǐ	10
泉	（名）	quán	7
缺少	（动）	quēshǎo	7
		R	
嚷	（动）	rǎng	9
热泪盈眶		rèlèi yíng kuàng	10
热烈	（形）	rèliè	10
人体	（名）	réntǐ	7
人为	（形）	rénwéi	8
人物	（名）	rénwù	6
任何	（代）	rènhé	4
任意	（副）	rènyì	1
如今	（名）	rújīn	10
		S	
沙子	（名）	shāzi	8
山泉	（名）	shānquán	7
上等	（形）	shàngděng	7
上涨	（动）	shàngzhǎng	3
设备	（名）	shèbèi	6
伸	（动）	shēn	2
身材	（名）	shēncái	3
深	（形）	shēn	2
深情	（形、名）	shēnqíng	4
神经病	（名）	shénjīngbìng	9
生分	（形）	shēngfen	5
失眠	（动）	shīmián	9
失业	（动）	shīyè	3
石雕	（名）	shídiāo	8
石窟	（名）	shíkū	8
时代	（名）	shídài	5
时髦	（形）	shímáo	2
实践	（动）	shíjiàn	9
实时	（副）	shíshí	10
世代	（名）	shìdài	9
世世代代		shìshìdàidài	9
收获	（名）	shōuhuò	10
收入	（名）	shōurù	8
收听	（动）	shōutīng	10
手续	（名）	shǒuxù	9
手指	（名）	shǒuzhǐ	4
首		shǒu	3
首都	（名）	shǒudū	3
蔬菜	（名）	shūcài	6
数目	（名）	shùmù	6
水面	（名）	shuǐmiàn	7
税	（名）	shuì	10
顺	（动）	shùn	2
顺路	（形）	shùnlù	2
说明	（动）	shuōmíng	4
似	（动）	sì	6
酥油	（名）	sūyóu	7
酥油茶	（名）	sūyóuchá	7
随	（动）	suí	3
孙子	（名）	sūnzi	10
		T	
塔	（名）	tǎ	3
弹	（动）	tán	8
坦率	（形）	tǎnshuài	10
掏	（动）	tāo	2
讨论	（动）	tǎolùn	5
讨厌	（动）	tǎoyàn	4
提醒	（动）	tíxǐng	9
题目	（名）	tímù	1
调	（动）	tiáo	9

通过	（介）	tōngguò	10
同时	（名、连）	tóngshí	5
同样	（形）	tóngyàng	2
痛	（形）	tòng	4
痛快	（形）	tòngkuai	9
头发	（名）	tóufa	3
拖拉	（形）	tuōlā	9
脱	（动）	tuō	4
W			
外人	（名）	wàirén	9
弯	（形）	wān	3
完好	（形）	wánhǎo	8
万一	（连）	wànyī	10
网络	（名）	wǎngluò	6
往常	（名）	wǎngcháng	10
往往	（副）	wǎngwǎng	5
危险	（形）	wēixiǎn	9
微笑	（动、名）	wēixiào	2
为	（动）	wéi	8
为人	（名）	wéirén	10
维生素	（名）	wéishēngsù	7
尾号	（名）	wěihào	10
文艺	（名）	wényì	9
吻	（动）	wěn	10
卧	（动）	wò	8
无	（动）	wú	4
无话不说		wúhuà-bùshuō	10
无价	（动）	wújià	4
无论如何		wúlùn-rúhé	3
无忧无虑		wúyōu-wúlǜ	10
五花八门		wǔhuā-bāmén	6
勿	（副）	wù	4
物价	（名）	wùjià	3

X			
喜爱	（动）	xǐ'ài	10
细	（形）	xì	6
下载	（动）	xiàzài	2
咸	（形）	xián	1
显得	（动）	xiǎnde	2
馅儿	（名）	xiànr	1
乡	（名）	xiāng	4
相处	（动）	xiāngchǔ	9
相同	（形）	xiāngtóng	1
享受	（动）	xiǎngshòu	7
想法	（名）	xiǎngfa	1
向导	（名）	xiàngdǎo	8
巷	（名）	xiàng	6
项目	（名）	xiàngmù	6
消化	（动）	xiāohuà	7
消失	（动）	xiāoshī	2
消息	（名）	xiāoxi	1
小康	（形）	xiǎokāng	5
效果	（名）	xiàoguǒ	4
心烦	（形）	xīnfán	9
心里	（名）	xīnli	9
心情	（名）	xīnqíng	9
心事	（名）	xīnshì	9
辛苦	（形）	xīnkǔ	4
辛劳	（形）	xīnláo	10
新郎	（名）	xīnláng	10
新娘	（名）	xīnniáng	10
新鲜	（形）	xīnxian	6
信息	（名）	xìnxī	7
行动	（动）	xíngdòng	1
形	（名）	xíng	1
形状	（名）	xíngzhuàng	1
幸亏	（副）	xìngkuī	9

秀气	(形)	xiùqi	3
绣	(动)	xiù	4
宣传	(动)	xuānchuán	10
宣传语	(名)	xuānchuányǔ	10
选择	(动)	xuǎnzé	1
Y			
牙齿	(名)	yáchǐ	3
轧	(动)	yà	4
演员	(名)	yǎnyuán	5
宴会	(名)	yànhuì	8
阳台	(名)	yángtái	3
药膏	(名)	yàogāo	4
医生	(名)	yīshēng	4
医学	(名)	yīxué	7
一下子	(副)	yíxiàzi	5
一致	(副)	yízhì	5
以	(介)	yǐ	6
一连	(副)	yìlián	9
一衣带水		yìyīdàishuǐ	9
艺术	(名)	yìshù	5
音节	(名)	yīnjié	5
音译	(动)	yīnyì	7
引起	(动)	yǐnqǐ	6
饮茶	(动)	yǐnchá	7
印象	(名)	yìnxiàng	2
硬	(形)	yìng	7
硬币	(名)	yìngbì	7
由于	(介、连)	yóuyú	6
油条	(名)	yóutiáo	1
友好	(形)	yǒuhǎo	9
有关	(介、动)	yǒuguān	6
于	(介)	yú	7
语文	(名)	yǔwén	5
原谅	(动)	yuánliàng	9

约	(副)	yuē	8
越来越……		yuè lái yuè…	6
Z			
脏	(形)	zāng	6
早茶	(名)	zǎochá	1
早出晚归		zǎochū-wǎnguī	10
炸	(动)	zhá	1
炸糕	(名)	zhágāo	1
窄	(形)	zhǎi	6
涨	(动)	zhǎng	3
招待	(动)	zhāodài	1
招待会	(名)	zhāodàihuì	1
招手	(动)	zhāoshǒu	2
召开	(动)	zhàokāi	4
着呢	(助)	zhene	3
真诚	(形)	zhēnchéng	10
真情	(名)	zhēnqíng	10
镇	(名)	zhèn	3
征求	(动)	zhēngqiú	5
正	(形)	zhèng	6
正巧	(副)	zhèngqiǎo	4
支撑	(动)	zhīchēng	10
直	(副)	zhí	2
止痛膏	(名)	zhǐtònggāo	4
指	(动)	zhǐ	3
至	(动)	zhì	5
至今	(副)	zhìjīn	5
衷心	(形)	zhōngxīn	4
种类	(名)	zhǒnglèi	1
种植	(动)	zhòngzhí	7
重视	(动)	zhòngshì	5
周岁	(名)	zhōusuì	5
主持	(动)	zhǔchí	6

主持人	（名）	zhǔchírén	6
嘱咐	（动）	zhǔfu	4
注册	（动）	zhùcè	2
祝福	（动）	zhùfú	10
著名	（形）	zhùmíng	3
专家	（名）	zhuānjiā	7
赚	（动）	zhuàn	10
撞	（动）	zhuàng	10
仔细	（形）	zǐxì	8
自	（介）	zì	5
自从	（介）	zìcóng	5
自来水	（名）	zìláishuǐ	7
自然	（名、形）	zìrán	8
自我	（代）	zìwǒ	4
总之	（连）	zǒngzhī	7
粽子	（名）	zòngzi	1
走廊	（名）	zǒuláng	9
租	（动）	zū	3
嘴唇	（名）	zuǐchún	3
尊敬	（动、形）	zūnjìng	5
作用	（名）	zuòyòng	6
做法	（名）	zuòfa	10

专名　Proper nouns

A		
安徽	Ānhuī	7
安娜	Ānnà	9
B		
北京饭店	Běijīng Fàndiàn	2
北京外国语大学	Běijīng Wàiguóyǔ Dàxué	3
D		
大同	Dàtóng	8
大雁塔	Dàyàn Tǎ	3
滴滴	Dīdī	2
F		
费城	Fèichéng	3
福建	Fújiàn	7
G		
国庆节	Guóqìngjié	8
H		
和平路	Hépíng Lù	2
虎跑泉	Hǔpǎo Quán	7
黄山	Huáng Shān	7
J		
吉姆	Jímǔ	4
加利福尼亚	Jiālìfúníyà	3
旧金山	Jiùjīnshān	3
K		
孔鲤	Kǒng Lǐ	5
孔子	Kǒngzǐ	5
L		
老舍	Lǎo Shě	7
卢京生	Lú Jīngshēng	10
M		
明（朝）	Míng (cháo)	6

N		
内蒙古	Nèiměnggǔ	7
纽约	Niǔyuē	3
Q		
钱塘江	Qiántáng Jiāng	3
清（朝）	Qīng (cháo)	6
S		
山西	Shānxī	8
上帝	Shàngdì	9
宋英	Sòng Yīng	8
T		
泰国	Tàiguó	7
吐鲁番	Tǔlǔfān	8
W		
王小康	Wáng Xiǎokāng	5
王学艺	Wáng Xuéyì	5
王志强	Wáng Zhìqiáng	5
武周山	Wǔzhōu Shān	8
X		
西藏	Xīzàng	7
希尔顿饭店	Xī'ěrdùn Fàndiàn	10
徐春兰	Xú Chūnlán	2
Y		
依丽拉	Yīlìlā	8
英国	Yīngguó	4
元朝	Yuáncháo	6
云冈石窟	Yúngāng Shíkū	8
云南	Yúnnán	7
Z		
中华人民共和国	Zhōnghuá Rénmín Gònghéguó	8
朱佳	Zhū Jiā	2

Glossary of Volume 1-Volume 5
第1—5册词汇总表

A			
阿		ā	4-7
阿姨	（名）	āyí	4-7
啊	（叹）	ā	2-6
啊	（叹）	à	3-5
啊	（助）	a	4-1
哎	（叹）	āi	4-1
哎呀	（叹）	āiyā	2-6
矮	（形）	ǎi	5-2
爱	（动）	ài	5-2
爱好	（名）	àihào	3-6
爱面子		ài miànzi	5-10
爱情	（名）	àiqíng	5-4
爱人	（名）	àiren	3-2
安静	（形）	ānjìng	5-3
安全	（形）	ānquán	4-9
安慰	（动）	ānwèi	5-8
按	（介）	àn	3-8
按时	（副）	ànshí	3-4
按照	（介）	ànzhào	3-8
B			
八	（数）	bā	1-1
把	（量）	bǎ	3-7
把	（介）	bǎ	4-8
爸爸	（名）	bàba	1-9
吧	（助）	ba	1-4
白	（形）	bái	1-9
白酒	（名）	báijiǔ	4-6
白天	（名）	báitiān	3-2
白头到老		báitóu-dàolǎo	3-10
百	（数）	bǎi	3-2
班	（名）	bān	2-2
搬	（动）	bān	3-7
办	（动）	bàn	1-10
办法	（名）	bànfǎ	1-7
办公	（动）	bàngōng	2-1
办公室	（名）	bàngōngshì	3-8
半	（数）	bàn	2-8
半天	（数量）	bàntiān	2-10
帮	（动）	bāng	1-4
帮忙	（动）	bāngmáng	5-1
帮助	（动）	bāngzhù	1-8
包	（动）	bāo	3-5
包裹	（名）	bāoguǒ	3-5
包装	（名、动）	bāozhuāng	3-5
饱	（形）	bǎo	5-3
保存	（动）	bǎocún	5-3
保龄球	（名）	bǎolíngqiú	4-5
保卫	（动）	bǎowèi	5-8
保卫处	（名）	bǎowèichù	5-8
保证	（动）	bǎozhèng	4-4
保证书	（名）	bǎozhèngshū	4-4
保质期	（名）	bǎozhìqī	5-3
报	（名）	bào	3-5
报名	（动）	bàomíng	4-1
报站	（动）	bàozhàn	5-6
报纸	（名）	bàozhǐ	4-10
抱	（动）	bào	4-8
抱歉	（形）	bàoqiàn	4-2

杯	（量）	bēi	3-6
杯子	（名）	bēizi	5-1
背	（动）	bēi	4-8
北	（名）	běi	3-1
北方	（名）	běifāng	3-5
北门	（名）	běimén	3-1
北面	（名）	běimiàn	4-2
背	（名）	bèi	5-8
倍	（量）	bèi	5-6
被	（介）	bèi	5-5
辈子	（名）	bèizi	5-7
奔	（动）	bēn	5-4
本	（量）	běn	2-2
本	（代）	běn	4-4
本子	（名）	běnzi	2-2
笨	（形）	bèn	5-10
鼻子	（名）	bízi	2-9
比	（动）	bǐ	3-1
比	（介）	bǐ	5-2
比价	（名）	bǐjià	3-8
比较	（副）	bǐjiào	1-10
比较	（动）	bǐjiào	4-5
比如	（动）	bǐrú	5-2
比赛	（动）	bǐsài	3-1
笔	（名）	bǐ	2-2
笔记本	（名）	bǐjìběn	3-10
笔记本电脑		bǐjìběn diànnǎo	3-10
笔试	（动）	bǐshì	1-10
必	（副）	bì	4-10
必须	（副）	bìxū	4-10
毕业	（动）	bìyè	4-4
变	（动）	biàn	5-2
变化	（名）	biànhuà	5-2
遍	（动、量）	biàn	4-3

表	（名）	biǎo	1-6
表示	（动）	biǎoshì	4-10
表演	（动）	biǎoyǎn	3-9
表扬	（动）	biǎoyáng	4-2
别	（副）	bié	1-6
别的	（代）	biéde	3-9
别人	（代）	biéren	2-9
宾馆	（名）	bīnguǎn	2-3
兵	（名）	bīng	4-3
兵马俑	（名）	bīngmǎyǒng	4-3
并	（副）	bìng	4-6
并	（连）	bìng	5-8
并且	（连）	bìngqiě	5-8
病	（动）	bìng	2-9
病房	（名）	bìngfáng	4-8
病人	（名）	bìngrén	4-10
玻璃	（名）	bōli	3-3
博士	（名）	bóshì	5-6
不错	（形）	búcuò	2-8
不但	（连）	búdàn	4-1
不断	（副）	búduàn	3-10
不对	（形）	búduì	2-1
不过	（连）	búguò	2-8
不见不散		bújiàn-búsàn	4-2
不是……就是……		bú shì… jiù shì…	4-9
不用	（副）	búyòng	2-7
不	（副）	bù	1-3
不得了	（形）	bùdéliǎo	4-8
不好意思		bù hǎoyìsi	3-7
不巧		bù qiǎo	3-8
不如	（动）	bùrú	5-4
部		bù	4-10

部分	（名）	bùfen	3-5
		C	
擦	（动）	cā	3-8
猜	（动）	cāi	2-1
才	（副）	cái	2-8
菜	（名）	cài	1-4
菜	（名）	cài	2-8
菜单	（名）	càidān	4-6
菜地	（名）	càidì	2-8
菜名儿	（名）	càimíngr	4-5
参观	（动）	cānguān	4-3
参加	（动）	cānjiā	3-3
餐厅	（名）	cāntīng	3-6
操场	（名）	cāochǎng	3-3
草	（名）	cǎo	4-10
草坪	（名）	cǎopíng	5-4
草原	（名）	cǎoyuán	5-8
册		cè	2-2
厕所	（名）	cèsuǒ	1-5
层	（量）	céng	2-3
曾	（副）	céng	4-3
曾经	（副）	céngjīng	4-3
茶	（名）	chá	2-9
茶几	（名）	chájī	4-7
茶具	（名）	chájù	3-3
茶叶	（名）	cháyè	3-3
查	（动）	chá	3-7
差	（动）	chà	3-1
差不多	（副）	chàbuduō	4-5
产品	（名）	chǎnpǐn	3-9
长	（形）	cháng	2-7
长度	（名）	chángdù	5-6
长期	（形）	chángqī	3-10
长寿	（形）	chángshòu	2-7
肠	（名）	cháng	4-10
肠胃炎	（名）	chángwèiyán	4-10
尝	（动）	cháng	2-9
常	（副）	cháng	1-6
场	（名、量）	chǎng	3-1
唱歌	（动）	chànggē	2-7
超市	（名）	chāoshì	1-6
超重	（动）	chāozhòng	3-5
炒	（动）	chǎo	4-6
车	（名）	chē	2-8
车站	（名）	chēzhàn	3-3
衬衫	（名）	chènshān	3-9
成	（动）	chéng	1-8
成功	（动）	chénggōng	4-4
成绩	（名）	chéngjì	3-2
成为	（动）	chéngwéi	5-5
诚信	（形）	chéngxìn	4-2
承认	（动）	chéngrèn	5-10
城	（名）	chéng	2-10
城市	（名）	chéngshì	2-10
吃	（动）	chī	1-4
吃苦	（动）	chīkǔ	5-7
迟到	（动）	chídào	3-7
充电器	（名）	chōngdiànqì	1-6
充分	（形）	chōngfèn	3-9
充满	（动）	chōngmǎn	5-6
重新	（副）	chóngxīn	3-5
抽	（动）	chōu	4-4
抽屉	（名）	chōuti	4-9
出	（动）	chū	2-4
出版	（动）	chūbǎn	3-6
出发	（动）	chūfā	3-1
出生	（动）	chūshēng	2-6
出院	（动）	chūyuàn	4-10

出租	（动）	chūzū	2-8
出租车	（名）	chūzūchē	2-8
初		chū	5-7
厨房	（名）	chúfáng	4-7
除了……以外		chúle…yǐwài	3-10
处	（名）	chù	5-5
穿	（动）	chuān	3-7
穿	（动）	chuān	5-6
穿越	（动）	chuānyuè	5-5
传说	（名）	chuánshuō	5-4
传统	（形）	chuántǒng	5-4
船	（名）	chuán	4-3
窗户	（名）	chuānghu	3-8
床	（名）	chuáng	1-6
创造	（动）	chuàngzào	5-5
吹	（动）	chuī	3-10
吹牛	（动）	chuīniú	4-8
春季	（名）	chūnjì	3-2
春天	（名）	chūntiān	3-2
词	（名）	cí	1-5
词典	（名）	cídiǎn	2-2
此	（代）	cǐ	5-9
次	（量）	cì	2-4
匆匆忙忙		cōngcōngmáng-máng	4-2
匆忙	（形）	cōngmáng	4-2
聪明	（形）	cōngming	2-4
从	（介）	cóng	2-9
从此	（副）	cóngcǐ	5-9
从来	（副）	cónglái	4-6
从前	（名）	cóngqián	5-7
粗心	（形）	cūxīn	4-9
催	（动）	cuī	5-9
村（子）	（名）	cūn(zi)	5-7

存	（动）	cún	3-8
存折	（名）	cúnzhé	5-9
错	（形）	cuò	1-5
错误	（名）	cuòwù	5-10
D			
答应	（动）	dāying	4-5
答案	（名）	dá'àn	5-2
打	（动）	dǎ	2-9
打扮	（动）	dǎban	5-1
打的	（动）	dǎdī	4-4
打电话		dǎ diànhuà	3-1
打开	（动）	dǎkāi	3-5
打篮球		dǎ lánqiú	3-8
打扫	（动）	dǎsǎo	2-6
打算	（动）	dǎsuàn	5-2
打太极拳		dǎ tàijíquán	3-10
打招呼		dǎ zhāohu	5-3
打折	（动）	dǎzhé	3-3
打着灯笼也难找		dǎzhe dēnglong yě nán zhǎo	4-8
打针	（动）	dǎzhēn	2-9
打字	（动）	dǎzì	4-1
大	（形）	dà	2-3
大便	（动、名）	dàbiàn	3-4
大概	（副）	dàgài	5-10
大家	（代）	dàjiā	3-7
大寿	（名）	dàshòu	5-7
大熊猫	（名）	dàxióngmāo	4-3
大学	（名）	dàxué	2-1
大约	（副）	dàyuē	4-9
呆	（形）	dāi	5-4
大夫	（名）	dàifu	2-1
代	（名）	dài	4-8
代	（动）	dài	4-9

代表	(动、名)	dàibiǎo	2-7
代替	(动)	dàitì	5-6
带	(动)	dài	2-8
戴	(动)	dài	5-2
单	(形)	dān	2-2
单车	(名)	dānchē	4-9
单间	(名)	dānjiān	5-7
单人间	(名)	dānrénjiān	2-3
单位	(名)	dānwèi	5-1
单子	(名)	dānzi	3-8
耽误	(动)	dānwu	3-1
但	(连)	dàn	3-10
但是	(连)	dànshì	3-10
蛋	(名)	dàn	5-7
蛋糕	(名)	dàngāo	2-6
当	(动)	dāng	2-5
当地	(名)	dāngdì	4-5
当然	(副)	dāngrán	2-8
当时	(名)	dāngshí	4-2
当作	(动)	dàngzuò	4-10
倒	(动)	dǎo	5-8
倒霉	(形)	dǎoméi	5-9
到	(动)	dào	1-8
到处	(副)	dàochù	2-9
到达	(动)	dàodá	5-5
到底	(副)	dàodǐ	5-10
到期	(动)	dàoqī	5-2
倒	(副)	dào	4-4
道	(量)	dào	5-5
道理	(名)	dàolǐ	5-3
道路	(名)	dàolù	5-6
道歉	(动)	dàoqiàn	4-2
得到	(动)	dédào	5-1
地	(助)	de	3-10

的	(助)	de	1-4
的话	(助)	dehuà	4-9
得	(助)	de	2-6
得	(能动)	děi	1-7
灯	(名)	dēng	4-8
灯笼	(名)	dēnglong	4-8
登	(动)	dēng	5-5
等	(动)	děng	2-10
等	(助)	děng	5-4
等待	(动)	děngdài	5-4
低	(形)	dī	3-2
的确	(副)	díquè	4-6
地	(名)	dì	2-8
地点	(名)	dìdiǎn	4-1
地方	(名)	dìfang	2-8
地理	(名)	dìlǐ	4-8
地球	(名)	dìqiú	5-5
地毯	(名)	dìtǎn	4-7
地铁	(名)	dìtiě	4-4
地图	(名)	dìtú	2-2
地下	(名)	dìxià	4-4
地址	(名)	dìzhǐ	5-9
弟弟	(名)	dìdi	2-1
递	(动)	dì	5-6
第		dì	4-2
点	(量)	diǎn	2-4
点	(动)	diǎn	4-4
点头	(动)	diǎntóu	5-10
点心	(名)	diǎnxin	3-6
电	(名)	diàn	2-8
电车	(名)	diànchē	4-4
电灯	(名)	diàndēng	4-8
电动车	(名)	diàndòngchē	5-8
电话	(名)	diànhuà	3-1

电脑	（名）	diànnǎo	3-10
电扇	（名）	diànshàn	3-4
电视	（名）	diànshì	3-10
电视机	（名）	diànshìjī	5-9
电影	（名）	diànyǐng	2-8
电影院	（名）	diànyǐngyuàn	2-8
店	（名）	diàn	5-3
掉	（动）	diào	4-4
丁	（名）	dīng	4-6
丁字路口		dīngzì lùkǒu	4-9
顶	（名）	dǐng	3-8
顶	（量）	dǐng	5-2
订	（动）	dìng	2-3
定	（动）	dìng	3-8
丢	（动）	diū	4-9
东	（名）	dōng	3-1
东方	（名）	dōngfāng	3-6
东面	（名）	dōngmiàn	4-2
东坡肉	（名）	dōngpōròu	4-5
东西	（名）	dōngxi	2-6
冬季	（名）	dōngjì	2-3
冬天	（名）	dōngtiān	2-3
懂	（动）	dǒng	2-4
动身	（动）	dòngshēn	4-3
动物	（名）	dòngwù	4-3
动物园	（名）	dòngwùyuán	4-3
动作	（名）	dòngzuò	2-6
都	（副）	dōu	1-9
读	（动）	dú	1-5
肚子	（名）	dùzi	2-9
度	（量）	dù	3-2
度过	（动）	dùguò	3-10
端	（动）	duān	4-7
短	（形）	duǎn	3-10

短期	（形）	duǎnqī	3-10
短信	（名）	duǎnxìn	5-8
段	（量）	duàn	5-5
断	（动）	duàn	5-8
锻炼	（动）	duànliàn	5-6
队	（名）	duì	3-1
对	（形）	duì	2-1
对	（介）	duì	2-5
对	（动）	duì	3-1
对不起	（动）	duìbuqǐ	1-5
对面	（名）	duìmiàn	3-2
对象	（名）	duìxiàng	5-1
兑换	（动）	duìhuàn	3-8
炖牛肉	（名）	dùnniúròu	1-4
顿	（量）	dùn	5-7
多	（形）	duō	1-6
多	（副）	duō	2-7
多少	（代）	duōshao	2-2
多子多福		duōzǐ duōfú	4-8
E			
饿	（形）	è	4-9
儿子	（名）	érzi	2-4
而	（连）	ér	5-5
而且	（连）	érqiě	4-1
耳环	（名）	ěrhuán	5-9
二	（数）	èr	1-1
二环路		èr-huánlù	4-9
F			
发	（动）	fā	2-1
发达	（形）	fādá	5-6
发烧	（动）	fāshāo	2-9
发生	（动）	fāshēng	5-8
发现	（动）	fāxiàn	5-1

发言	(动、名)	fāyán	3-7
发炎	(动)	fāyán	3-4
发音	(名)	fāyīn	1-10
发展	(动)	fāzhǎn	5-10
法律	(名)	fǎlǜ	3-8
翻译	(名)	fānyì	2-5
反正	(副)	fǎnzhèng	5-10
饭	(名)	fàn	1-4
饭店	(名)	fàndiàn	4-5
饭馆儿	(名)	fànguǎnr	4-5
方便	(形)	fāngbiàn	2-4
方法	(名)	fāngfǎ	1-10
方面	(名)	fāngmiàn	2-5
方向	(名)	fāngxiàng	4-9
房	(名)	fáng	4-7
房间	(名)	fángjiān	2-3
访问	(动)	fǎngwèn	4-3
放	(动)	fàng	4-2
放假	(动)	fàngjià	5-6
放心	(动)	fàngxīn	3-1
飞	(动)	fēi	4-6
飞船	(名)	fēichuán	5-4
飞机	(名)	fēijī	3-4
飞快	(形)	fēikuài	5-10
非	(动)	fēi	5-5
非常	(副)	fēicháng	2-6
肥	(形)	féi	4-5
费	(名)	fèi	3-5
分	(量)	fēn	3-1
分别	(动)	fēnbié	5-9
风	(名)	fēng	3-4
风味	(名)	fēngwèi	4-5
封	(量)	fēng	2-1
否认	(动)	fǒurèn	5-10

夫妇	(名)	fūfù	4-7
服务	(动)	fúwù	2-3
服务员	(名)	fúwùyuán	2-3
幅	(量)	fú	2-6
福	(名)	fú	4-7
抚摸	(动)	fǔmō	5-5
斧子	(名)	fǔzi	5-9
辅导	(动)	fǔdǎo	2-4
父母	(名)	fùmǔ	5-2
父亲	(名)	fùqin	3-2
付	(动)	fù	2-2
附件	(名)	fùjiàn	3-10
附近	(名)	fùjìn	1-5
复习	(动)	fùxí	1-7
副	(形)	fù	2-1
富有	(动)	fùyǒu	4-1
腹	(名)	fù	4-10
腹泻	(动)	fùxiè	4-10
G			
该	(能动)	gāi	1-9
改	(动)	gǎi	5-10
改变	(动)	gǎibiàn	3-9
改进	(动)	gǎijìn	3-7
改善	(动)	gǎishàn	5-6
改正	(动)	gǎizhèng	5-10
干净	(形)	gānjìng	2-6
敢	(能动)	gǎn	4-6
感到	(动)	gǎndào	5-2
感动	(形)	gǎndòng	4-2
感冒	(名、动)	gǎnmào	3-4
感受	(名)	gǎnshòu	5-7
感谢	(动)	gǎnxiè	2-5
干	(动)	gàn	4-1
干吗	(代)	gànmá	3-8

刚	（副）	gāng	2-2
刚才	（名）	gāngcái	4-4
钢笔	（名）	gāngbǐ	2-2
高	（形）	gāo	3-2
高大	（形）	gāodà	5-8
高尔夫球	（名）	gāo'ěrfūqiú	4-5
高铁	（名）	gāotiě	4-3
高兴	（形）	gāoxìng	1-8
告诉	（动）	gàosu	3-8
哥哥	（名）	gēge	1-9
歌曲	（名）	gēqǔ	3-10
隔	（动）	gé	4-7
个	（量）	gè	1-8
个子	（名）	gèzi	4-8
各	（代）	gè	4-3
给	（动）	gěi	1-3
给	（介）	gěi	2-1
给	（助）	gěi	5-9
跟	（介）	gēn	1-10
更换	（动）	gēnghuàn	5-3
更	（副）	gèng	2-4
工厂	（名）	gōngchǎng	2-1
工程	（名）	gōngchéng	5-10
工程师	（名）	gōngchéngshī	5-10
工地	（名）	gōngdì	5-10
工人	（名）	gōngrén	2-1
工作	（名）	gōngzuò	2-1
公安	（名）	gōng'ān	5-9
公安局	（名）	gōng'ānjú	5-9
公分	（量）	gōngfēn	5-2
公共	（形）	gōnggòng	2-8
公共汽车		gōnggòng qìchē	2-8
公斤	（量）	gōngjīn	5-2
公里	（量）	gōnglǐ	5-2

公司	（名）	gōngsī	2-1
公务员	（名）	gōngwùyuán	2-5
公园儿	（名）	gōngyuánr	1-9
宫保鸡丁		gōngbǎo jīdīng	4-6
共	（副）	gòng	4-1
共同	（副、形）	gòngtóng	3-10
共享	（动）	gòngxiǎng	4-9
共享单车		gòngxiǎng dānchē	4-9
贡献	（名）	gòngxiàn	4-3
狗	（名）	gǒu	2-1
够	（动）	gòu	3-9
估计	（动）	gūjì	5-6
姑姑	（名）	gūgu	4-7
姑娘	（名）	gūniang	2-9
古	（形）	gǔ	5-8
古代	（名）	gǔdài	5-2
古迹	（名）	gǔjì	4-3
古老	（形）	gǔlǎo	3-6
故事	（名）	gùshi	3-8
瓜	（名）	guā	5-3
刮风	（动）	guāfēng	3-4
挂	（动）	guà	4-7
挂号	（动）	guàhào	3-5
拐	（动）	guǎi	4-9
怪	（形）	guài	2-6
怪不得	（副）	guàibude	2-6
关	（动）	guān	2-7
关	（名）	guān	5-5
关系	（名）	guānxi	2-6
关心	（动）	guānxīn	3-7
关于	（介）	guānyú	4-3
关照	（动）	guānzhào	4-5
关注	（动）	guānzhù	3-3

观点	（名）	guāndiǎn	5-10
观念	（名）	guānniàn	4-8
观众	（名）	guānzhòng	3-1
管	（名、动）	guǎn	4-8
罐头	（名）	guàntou	5-6
光	（副）	guāng	5-2
光	（名）	guāng	5-4
广播	（动、名）	guǎngbō	4-1
逛	（动）	guàng	2-10
规定	（名）	guīdìng	3-8
柜子	（名）	guìzi	5-9
贵	（形）	guì	1-3
贵姓	（名）	guìxìng	1-3
国	（名）	guó	1-4
国产	（形）	guóchǎn	3-3
国际	（形）	guójì	5-1
国家	（名）	guójiā	3-2
果园	（名）	guǒyuán	2-8
果汁儿	（名）	guǒzhīr	4-6
过	（动）	guò	2-7
过错	（名）	guòcuò	4-4
过去	（名）	guòqù	4-8
过	（助）	guo	4-3
		H	
哈哈	（叹）	hāhā	1-6
还	（副）	hái	1-7
还是	（连）	háishi	2-3
还是	（副）	háishi	2-10
孩子	（名）	háizi	2-10
海	（名）	hǎi	3-5
海棠	（名）	hǎitáng	5-4
海运	（动）	hǎiyùn	3-5
喊	（动）	hǎn	2-7
汉学	（名）	hànxué	3-6

汗	（名）	hàn	4-6
行家	（名）	hángjia	3-3
航空	（动）	hángkōng	3-5
好	（形）	hǎo	1-1
好吃	（形）	hǎochī	2-3
好处	（名）	hǎochù	2-10
好汉	（名）	hǎohàn	5-5
好几	（数）	hǎojǐ	5-1
好久	（形）	hǎojiǔ	1-7
好看	（形）	hǎokàn	1-9
好像	（副）	hǎoxiàng	3-6
号	（名）	hào	2-3
号码	（名）	hàomǎ	4-2
好	（动）	hào	5-1
喝	（动）	hē	1-3
合	（动）	hé	2-10
合格	（形）	hégé	5-3
合理	（形）	hélǐ	5-3
合适	（形）	héshì	2-3
合影	（名）	héyǐng	4-7
合住	（动）	hézhù	2-10
和	（连、介）	hé	1-9
河	（名）	hé	2-8
盒儿	（名）	hér	4-4
盒子	（名）	hézi	5-3
贺卡	（名）	hèkǎ	3-5
黑板	（名）	hēibǎn	2-2
很	（副）	hěn	1-4
红	（形）	hóng	1-9
红茶	（名）	hóngchá	3-3
红绿灯	（名）	hóng-lǜdēng	4-9
红烧	（动）	hóngshāo	4-5
红烧猪手		hóngshāo zhūshǒu	4-5
猴	（名）	hóu	2-6

后	(名)	hòu	2-8
后边	(名)	hòubian	2-8
后代	(名)	hòudài	5-5
后来	(名)	hòulái	3-8
后面	(名)	hòumiàn	4-2
后年	(名)	hòunián	3-2
后天	(名)	hòutiān	2-3
厚	(形)	hòu	5-3
忽然	(副)	hūrán	5-1
湖	(名)	hú	4-3
互相	(副)	hùxiāng	1-8
护士	(名)	hùshi	4-10
护照	(名)	hùzhào	3-8
花	(动)	huā	3-3
花草	(名)	huācǎo	4-10
花儿	(名)	huār	1-9
花生米	(名)	huāshēngmǐ	4-6
花园	(名)	huāyuán	4-10
划	(动)	huá	4-3
滑冰	(动)	huábīng	3-2
化验	(动)	huàyàn	3-4
画	(动)	huà	2-9
画报	(名)	huàbào	3-5
画儿	(名)	huàr	2-6
话	(名)	huà	2-7
话剧	(名)	huàjù	5-7
话题	(名)	huàtí	4-8
怀疑	(动)	huáiyí	5-9
坏	(形)	huài	5-8
欢快	(形)	huānkuài	5-6
欢迎	(动)	huānyíng	1-8
还	(动)	huán	3-8
环	(名)	huán	4-9
环境	(名)	huánjìng	2-8

环路	(名)	huánlù	4-9
换	(动)	huàn	3-8
黄	(形)	huáng	1-9
恢复	(动)	huīfù	2-9
回	(动)	huí	1-7
回	(量)	huí	3-8
会	(能动)	huì	2-8
会	(名)	huì	5-8
会议	(名)	huìyì	5-6
婚姻	(名)	hūnyīn	5-1
活	(形)	huó	5-1
活儿	(名)	huór	5-7
火车	(名)	huǒchē	4-3
伙伴	(名)	huǒbàn	5-9
或	(连)	huò	2-10
或者	(连)	huòzhě	2-10
货	(名)	huò	3-9
J			
几乎	(副)	jīhū	4-5
机场	(名)	jīchǎng	3-3
机会	(名)	jīhuì	3-7
机票	(名)	jīpiào	3-6
机器	(名)	jīqì	3-8
鸡	(名)	jī	4-6
鸡蛋	(名)	jīdàn	5-7
鸡丁	(名)	jīdīng	4-6
积极	(形)	jījí	3-7
基本	(形、副)	jīběn	5-10
基础	(名)	jīchǔ	3-8
激动	(形)	jīdòng	5-9
及格	(动)	jígé	3-4
及时	(副)	jíshí	5-4
吉利	(形)	jílì	2-7
级	(名)	jí	5-5

极	（副）	jí	1-7
极了		jí le	1-7
急	（形）	jí	4-8
急忙	（副）	jímáng	5-10
急事	（名）	jíshì	4-8
急性	（形）	jíxìng	4-10
急诊室	（名）	jízhěnshì	4-10
集邮	（动）	jíyóu	3-5
几	（代）	jǐ	2-1
挤	（形）	jǐ	2-10
记	（动）	jì	1-5
记得	（动）	jìde	4-5
纪律	（名）	jìlǜ	4-9
纪念	（动、名）	jìniàn	3-5
纪念品	（名）	jìniànpǐn	5-9
纪念日	（名）	jìniànrì	3-10
季	（名）	jì	3-2
季节	（名）	jìjié	3-2
既……也……		jì…yě…	4-9
既……又……		jì…yòu…	4-5
既然	（连）	jìrán	5-3
寄	（动）	jì	2-6
寄件人	（名）	jìjiànrén	5-9
寂寞	（形）	jìmò	4-10
加强	（动）	jiāqiáng	3-7
家	（名）	jiā	1-9
……家		…jiā	3-6
家庭	（名）	jiātíng	2-1
家务	（名）	jiāwù	4-8
假	（形）	jiǎ	2-10
价	（名）	jià	3-9
价格	（名）	jiàgé	3-9
价值	（名）	jiàzhí	3-9
架	（量）	jià	3-4
假日	（名）	jiàrì	4-3
间	（量）	jiān	4-7
肩	（名）	jiān	5-5
检查	（动）	jiǎnchá	4-10
减	（动）	jiǎn	5-6
减肥	（动）	jiǎnféi	5-6
减少	（动）	jiǎnshǎo	5-6
简单	（形）	jiǎndān	2-3
见	（动）	jiàn	1-6
见面	（动）	jiànmiàn	5-1
件	（量）	jiàn	2-3
建	（动）	jiàn	4-5
建议	（动）	jiànyì	3-6
建筑	（动、名）	jiànzhù	4-5
健康	（形）	jiànkāng	2-7
将	（副）	jiāng	4-1
讲	（动）	jiǎng	3-4
讲台	（名）	jiǎngtái	3-7
讲座	（名）	jiǎngzuò	4-1
交	（动）	jiāo	2-1
交换	（动）	jiāohuàn	2-4
交际	（动）	jiāojì	5-10
交通	（名）	jiāotōng	4-9
郊		jiāo	2-8
郊区	（名）	jiāoqū	2-8
教	（动）	jiāo	2-4
角	（量）	jiǎo	3-3
狡辩	（动）	jiǎobiàn	4-4
饺子	（名）	jiǎozi	4-1
叫	（动）	jiào	1-3
叫	（介）	jiào	5-9
叫号	（动）	jiàohào	3-8
教师	（名）	jiàoshī	2-5

教室	（名）	jiàoshì	2-4
教授	（名）	jiàoshòu	3-9
教学	（名）	jiàoxué	2-1
阶段	（名）	jiēduàn	2-4
接	（动）	jiē	2-10
接受	（动）	jiēshòu	4-2
接着	（副）	jiēzhe	5-5
街	（名）	jiē	2-8
节目	（名）	jiémù	3-9
结	（动）	jié	3-10
结果	（名）	jiéguǒ	3-4
结果	（连）	jiéguǒ	5-8
结婚	（动）	jiéhūn	3-6
结束	（动）	jiéshù	2-5
结账	（动）	jiézhàng	4-6
姐姐	（名）	jiějie	2-1
解饿	（动）	jiě'è	5-2
解渴	（动）	jiěkě	5-2
解释	（动）	jiěshì	5-9
介绍	（动）	jièshào	1-8
戒	（动）	jiè	4-4
戒指	（名）	jièzhi	5-9
借	（动）	jiè	3-6
斤	（量）	jīn	3-3
今年	（名）	jīnnián	2-9
今天	（名）	jīntiān	2-1
金	（名）	jīn	3-10
金婚	（名）	jīnhūn	3-10
金子	（名）	jīnzi	3-10
紧张	（形）	jǐnzhāng	1-7
尽力	（动）	jìnlì	5-1
尽头	（名）	jìntóu	5-5
进	（动）	jìn	2-6
进步	（动）	jìnbù	2-5

进口	（动）	jìnkǒu	3-3
进行	（动）	jìnxíng	2-5
近	（形）	jìn	1-5
京剧	（名）	jīngjù	3-8
经常	（副）	jīngcháng	3-6
经过	（动）	jīngguò	3-9
经济	（名）	jīngjì	5-7
经理	（名）	jīnglǐ	2-1
经历	（名）	jīnglì	5-6
经商	（动）	jīngshāng	2-5
惊叹号	（名）	jīngtànhào	5-5
精彩	（形）	jīngcǎi	5-3
精神	（形）	jīngshen	5-1
警察	（名）	jǐngchá	3-3
九	（数）	jiǔ	1-1
久	（形）	jiǔ	1-7
酒	（名）	jiǔ	3-6
酒店	（名）	jiǔdiàn	5-7
旧	（形）	jiù	3-4
救	（动）	jiù	5-1
就	（副）	jiù	2-2
舅舅	（名）	jiùjiu	4-7
舅妈	（名）	jiùmā	4-7
局	（名）	jú	5-9
橘子	（名）	júzi	5-3
举	（动）	jǔ	3-7
举办	（动）	jǔbàn	3-6
举行	（动）	jǔxíng	4-2
句	（名）	jù	1-10
句子	（名）	jùzi	1-10
剧场	（名）	jùchǎng	2-8
据	（介）	jù	5-6
卷	（量）	juǎn	5-10
觉得	（动）	juéde	1-10

决定	（动）	juédìng	4-4
K			
咖啡	（名）	kāfēi	4-1
卡拉OK		kǎlā OK	5-7
开	（动）	kāi	2-7
开会	（动）	kāihuì	5-8
开始	（动）	kāishǐ	2-4
开水	（名）	kāishuǐ	3-4
开玩笑		kāi wánxiào	3-6
开心	（形）	kāixīn	5-4
开学	（动）	kāixué	5-6
开演	（动）	kāiyǎn	4-6
看	（动）	kàn	1-6
看不起	（动）	kànbuqǐ	5-3
看来	（动）	kànlái	3-1
看望	（动）	kànwàng	4-9
看作	（动）	kànzuò	5-4
考	（动）	kǎo	3-4
考虑	（动）	kǎolǜ	2-3
考试	（动）	kǎoshì	3-4
烤	（动）	kǎo	4-3
烤鸭	（名）	kǎoyā	4-3
科	（名）	kē	4-10
棵	（量）	kē	4-10
咳嗽	（动）	késou	2-9
可	（连）	kě	1-10
可	（能动）	kě	5-8
可……了		kě…le	4-5
可爱	（形）	kě'ài	2-6
可能	（能动、名）	kěnéng	3-3
可是	（连）	kěshì	1-10
可以	（能动）	kěyǐ	2-2
渴	（形）	kě	1-3
克服	（动）	kèfú	5-1
刻	（量）	kè	3-1
刻苦	（形）	kèkǔ	5-1
客气	（动、形）	kèqi	1-8
客人	（名）	kèren	4-2
客厅	（名）	kètīng	4-7
课	（名）	kè	1-7
课本	（名）	kèběn	4-8
课间	（名）	kèjiān	4-9
课堂	（名）	kètáng	5-10
课文	（名）	kèwén	1-5
肯定	（副）	kěndìng	5-8
空气	（名）	kōngqì	5-1
空调	（名）	kōngtiáo	2-3
空运	（动）	kōngyùn	3-5
空儿	（名）	kòngr	1-8
空隙	（名）	kòngxì	5-6
口	（量）	kǒu	2-1
口袋	（名）	kǒudai	4-9
口感	（名）	kǒugǎn	3-3
口试	（动）	kǒushì	1-10
口语	（名）	kǒuyǔ	2-4
扣子	（名）	kòuzi	5-6
哭	（动）	kū	4-8
苦	（形）	kǔ	4-10
裤子	（名）	kùzi	3-9
夸奖	（动）	kuājiǎng	3-6
块	（量）	kuài	1-4
快	（形）	kuài	2-5
快递	（名）	kuàidì	4-9
快乐	（形）	kuàilè	2-7
筷子	（名）	kuàizi	3-8
宽	（形）	kuān	3-2
筐	（名）	kuāng	5-3

困	（形）	kùn	4-9
困难	（名）	kùnnan	5-1
L			
拉	（动）	lā	4-8
蜡烛	（名）	làzhú	2-6
辣	（形）	là	4-5
啦	（助）	la	2-6
来	（动）	lái	1-4
来	（名）	lái	5-5
来不及	（动）	láibují	3-8
来着	（助）	láizhe	5-7
栏	（名）	lán	5-9
蓝	（形）	lán	1-9
篮球	（名）	lánqiú	3-8
浪费	（动）	làngfèi	3-9
浪漫	（形）	làngmàn	4-1
劳驾	（动）	láojià	2-2
老		lǎo	2-4
老	（形）	lǎo	2-7
老板	（名）	lǎobǎn	3-3
老大爷	（名）	lǎodàye	5-6
老婆	（名）	lǎopo	5-1
老人	（名）	lǎorén	2-7
老师	（名）	lǎoshī	1-3
老是	（副）	lǎoshì	5-7
老实	（形）	lǎoshi	5-6
姥姥	（名）	lǎolao	4-7
姥爷	（名）	lǎoye	4-7
了	（助）	le	1-3
累	（形）	lèi	1-3
冷	（形）	lěng	2-3
离	（动）	lí	2-8
离婚	（动）	líhūn	4-4
礼堂	（名）	lǐtáng	5-6
礼物	（名）	lǐwù	2-6
里	（量）	lǐ	1-9
里	（名）	lǐ	1-9
里边	（名）	lǐbian	1-9
里面	（名）	lǐmiàn	4-2
理解	（动）	lǐjiě	5-2
理想	（名）	lǐxiǎng	5-5
力气	（名）	lìqi	5-3
历史	（名）	lìshǐ	2-5
厉害	（形）	lìhai	3-4
立交桥	（名）	lìjiāoqiáo	5-6
立刻	（副）	lìkè	5-8
利于	（动）	lìyú	4-10
俩	（数量）	liǎ	4-3
连	（动）	lián	3-10
连……也/都……		lián…yě/dōu…	4-6
连接	（动）	liánjiē	5-5
连忙	（副）	liánmáng	4-2
脸	（名）	liǎn	3-2
脸色	（名）	liǎnsè	3-2
练	（动）	liàn	1-7
练习	（名）	liànxí	1-7
恋爱	（名、动）	liàn'ài	5-7
良	（形）	liáng	4-10
良药苦口利于病		liángyào kǔkǒu lìyú bìng	4-10
凉快	（形）	liángkuai	2-3
量	（动）	liáng	3-4
两	（数）	liǎng	2-2
两	（量）	liǎng	3-3
亮	（形）	liàng	5-4
辆	（量）	liàng	3-6
聊天儿	（动）	<口>liáotiānr	2-5

了	（动）	liǎo	5-1
了解	（动）	liǎojiě	2-5
瞭望台	（名）	liàowàngtái	5-5
邻居	（名）	línjū	5-7
灵	（形）	líng	4-4
领	（动）	lǐng	5-8
领导	（名）	lǐngdǎo	5-3
另	（代）	lìng	5-2
另外	（连）	lìngwài	5-10
留	（动）	liú	4-3
留步	（动）	liúbù	4-2
留学	（动）	liúxué	2-5
留学生	（名）	liúxuéshēng	2-5
流利	（形）	liúlì	2-6
六	（数）	liù	1-1
龙	（名）	lóng	5-4
楼	（名）	lóu	1-8
录像	（动、名）	lùxiàng	5-7
录音	（名）	lùyīn	1-10
录音笔	（名）	lùyīnbǐ	3-4
路	（名）	lù	1-9
路口	（名）	lùkǒu	4-9
路上	（名）	lùshang	5-3
路线	（名）	lùxiàn	4-9
旅行	（动）	lǚxíng	2-5
旅行社	（名）	lǚxíngshè	5-1
旅游	（动）	lǚyóu	4-3
绿	（形）	lǜ	5-5
绿茶	（名）	lǜchá	3-3
轮	（量）	lún	5-4
M			
妈妈	（名）	māma	1-9
麻	（形）	má	4-6
麻烦	（动）	máfan	3-5
麻将	（名）	májiàng	5-7
马	（名）	mǎ	4-3
马路	（名）	mǎlù	4-9
马上	（副）	mǎshàng	4-7
骂	（动）	mà	4-8
吗	（助）	ma	1-3
嘛	（助）	ma	4-10
买	（动）	mǎi	1-6
买卖	（名）	mǎimai	5-3
卖	（动）	mài	3-3
馒头	（名）	mántou	1-4
满	（形）	mǎn	4-6
满意	（动）	mǎnyì	4-6
满足	（动）	mǎnzú	4-1
慢	（形）	màn	2-5
忙	（形）	máng	1-4
盲肠	（名）	mángcháng	4-10
盲肠炎	（名）	mángchángyán	4-10
毛	（量）	máo	3-3
毛病	（名）	máobìng	5-8
毛衣	（名）	máoyī	3-6
矛盾	（名、动）	máodùn	4-8
茅台酒	（名）	máotáijiǔ	3-6
冒	（动）	mào	4-1
帽子	（名）	màozi	5-2
没	（动）	méi	1-7
没关系		méi guānxi	2-6
没有	（动）	méiyǒu	1-7
每	（代）	měi	1-5
每天		měi tiān	1-5
美	（形）	měi	4-5
美好	（形）	měihǎo	3-10
美丽	（形）	měilì	5-4

美食城	（名）	měishíchéng	4-5
美食家	（名）	měishíjiā	4-5
美味佳肴		měiwèi jiāyáo	4-5
美元	（名）	měiyuán	2-3
妹妹	（名）	mèimei	2-1
门	（名）	mén	2-7
门口	（名）	ménkǒu	3-1
门诊部	（名）	ménzhěnbù	4-10
们		men	3-7
猛	（副）	měng	5-6
梦	（动、名）	mèng	4-7
梦想	（名）	mèngxiǎng	5-5
迷	（动）	mí	3-1
……迷		…mí	3-1
米	（量）	mǐ	3-2
米饭	（名）	mǐfàn	1-4
面包	（名）	miànbāo	3-6
面积	（名）	miànjī	5-6
面料	（名）	miànliào	3-9
面条儿	（名）	miàntiáor	4-1
面子	（名）	miànzi	5-10
秒	（量）	miǎo	3-2
民歌	（名）	míngē	5-4
民俗	（名）	mínsú	5-2
民族	（名）	mínzú	5-4
名牌儿	（名）	míngpáir	3-9
名片	（名）	míngpiàn	4-2
名儿	（名）	míngr	4-5
名胜	（名）	míngshèng	4-3
名字	（名）	míngzi	1-8
明白	（形）	míngbai	2-10
明亮	（形）	míngliàng	5-4
明码标价		míngmǎ biāojià	3-9
明年	（名）	míngnián	3-2
明天	（名）	míngtiān	1-9
明信片	（名）	míngxìnpiàn	3-5
命	（名）	mìng	4-9
摸	（动）	mō	4-9
模仿	（动）	mófǎng	5-10
摩托车	（名）	mótuōchē	5-8
某	（代）	mǒu	3-9
母亲	（名）	mǔqin	2-9
木		mù	4-10
目的	（名）	mùdì	2-5
N			
拿	（动）	ná	3-3
拿……来说		ná…lái shuō	4-5
拿手	（形）	náshǒu	4-6
哪	（代）	nǎ	1-4
哪里	（代）	nǎli	3-5
哪儿	（代）	nǎr	1-7
那	（代）	nà	1-5
那	（连）	nà	3-9
那边	（名）	nàbian	1-5
那里	（代）	nàlǐ	5-10
那么	（代）	nàme	1-9
那儿	（代）	nàr	1-6
那样	（代）	nàyàng	5-4
哪	（助）	na	4-1
奶	（名）	nǎi	5-2
奶奶	（名）	nǎinai	1-9
耐心	（形、名）	nàixīn	5-4
男	（形）	nán	1-5
男孩儿	（名）	nánháir	3-7
男人	（名）	〈口〉 nánren	4-8
男生	（名）	nánshēng	2-4
南	（名）	nán	3-1

南方	（名）	nánfāng	2-5
南门	（名）	nánmén	3-1
南面	（名）	nánmiàn	4-2
难	（形）	nán	1-10
难过	（形）	nánguò	5-9
闹	（动、形）	nào	5-9
闹钟	（名）	nàozhōng	5-9
呢	（助）	ne	1-4
内		nèi	4-10
内科	（名）	nèikē	4-10
内容	（名）	nèiróng	5-2
能	（能动）	néng	2-5
你	（代）	nǐ	1-1
你们	（代）	nǐmen	1-2
年	（名）	nián	2-6
年代	（名）	niándài	5-6
年级	（名）	niánjí	2-2
年纪	（名）	niánjì	2-4
年龄	（名）	niánlíng	2-9
年轻	（形）	niánqīng	2-4
念	（动）	niàn	1-5
您	（代）	nín	1-2
牛奶	（名）	niúnǎi	5-2
牛肉	（名）	niúròu	1-4
农历	（名）	nónglì	5-4
农贸市场		nóngmào shìchǎng	5-3
农民	（名）	nóngmín	5-8
弄	（动）	nòng	5-8
努力	（形）	nǔlì	3-2
暖和	（形）	nuǎnhuo	2-3
暖气	（名）	nuǎnqì	2-3
女	（形）	nǚ	1-5
女儿	（名）	nǚ'ér	2-4

女孩儿	（名）	nǚháir	3-7
女孩子	（名）	nǚháizi	2-9
女人	（名）	nǚrén	4-8
女生	（名）	nǚshēng	2-4
女士	（名）	nǚshì	3-9
P			
爬	（动）	pá	3-8
怕	（动）	pà	3-7
排球	（名）	páiqiú	4-5
牌子	（名）	páizi	5-10
派	（动）	pài	4-9
盘	（量）	pán	4-6
旁	（名）	páng	2-8
旁边	（名）	pángbiān	2-8
胖	（形）	pàng	4-1
跑	（动）	pǎo	2-6
陪	（动）	péi	4-7
朋友	（名）	péngyou	1-4
批	（量）	pī	3-9
批评	（动）	pīpíng	4-2
皮鞋	（名）	píxié	3-3
啤酒	（名）	píjiǔ	3-6
匹	（量）	pǐ	5-8
篇	（量）	piān	2-6
便宜	（形）	piányi	1-6
片	（名、量）	piàn	3-4
骗	（动）	piàn	3-3
票	（名）	piào	3-1
漂亮	（形）	piàoliang	2-7
……品		…pǐn	5-9
品尝	（动）	pǐncháng	4-5
聘请	（动）	pìnqǐng	4-1
乒乓球	（名）	pīngpāngqiú	4-5

平等	(形)	píngděng	4-8
平方	(名、量)	píngfāng	5-6
平方米	(量)	píngfāngmǐ	5-6
平时	(名)	píngshí	4-9
苹果	(名)	píngguǒ	2-3
瓶	(量)	píng	3-6
破	(形、动)	pò	5-3
破旧	(形)	pòjiù	5-3
扑克	(名)	pūkè	5-7
铺	(动)	pū	4-7
葡萄	(名)	pútao	4-6
葡萄酒	(名)	pútaojiǔ	4-6
普洱茶	(名)	pǔ'ěrchá	3-3
普通	(形)	pǔtōng	5-2
普通话	(名)	pǔtōnghuà	5-2
		Q	
七	(数)	qī	1-1
沏	(动)	qī	4-7
妻管严		qīguǎnyán	4-8
妻子	(名)	qīzi	3-6
期	(名)	qī	5-2
期间	(名)	qījiān	5-10
其实	(副)	qíshí	5-10
奇怪	(形)	qíguài	3-3
奇迹	(名)	qíjì	5-5
骑	(动)	qí	2-8
棋	(名)	qí	5-7
起床	(动)	qǐchuáng	3-1
气氛	(名)	qìfēn	5-6
气功	(名)	qìgōng	4-7
气管	(名)	qìguǎn	4-8
气管炎	(名)	qìguǎnyán	4-8
气温	(名)	qìwēn	3-2
汽车	(名)	qìchē	2-8
汽车站	(名)	qìchēzhàn	4-9
汽水儿	(名)	qìshuǐr	4-6
千	(数)	qiān	3-2
千儿八百		qiān'er-bābǎi	5-7
千万	(副)	qiānwàn	4-9
铅笔	(名)	qiānbǐ	2-2
谦虚	(形)	qiānxū	4-1
签字	(动)	qiānzì	3-8
前	(名)	qián	1-8
前边	(名)	qiánbian	1-8
前面	(名)	qiánmiàn	4-2
前年	(名)	qiánnián	3-2
前天	(名)	qiántiān	2-3
钱	(名)	qián	2-2
钱包	(名)	qiánbāo	2-8
强	(形)	qiáng	5-8
强调	(动)	qiángdiào	5-10
强壮	(形)	qiángzhuàng	5-8
墙	(名)	qiáng	2-8
敲	(动)	qiāo	2-7
桥	(名)	qiáo	3-7
瞧	(动)	qiáo	3-3
亲爱	(形)	qīn'ài	3-6
亲戚	(名)	qīnqi	5-7
亲人	(名)	qīnrén	4-10
青	(形)	qīng	4-6
青菜	(名)	qīngcài	4-6
轻	(形)	qīng	5-2
轻松	(形)	qīngsōng	4-2
清楚	(形)	qīngchu	2-6
清淡	(形)	qīngdàn	4-5
情况	(名)	qíngkuàng	1-8
情人	(名)	qíngrén	3-6
晴	(形)	qíng	3-2

晴朗	（形）	qínglǎng	5-4
请	（动）	qǐng	1-8
请假	（动）	qǐngjià	3-7
请客	（动）	qǐngkè	2-2
请问	（动）	qǐngwèn	1-8
庆祝	（动）	qìngzhù	3-6
秋季	（名）	qiūjì	3-2
秋天	（名）	qiūtiān	3-2
球	（名）	qiú	3-1
区		qū	2-10
取	（动）	qǔ	3-6
取得	（动）	qǔdé	3-7
娶	（动）	qǔ	5-7
去	（动）	qù	1-6
去年	（名）	qùnián	3-2
去世	（动）	qùshì	4-4
全	（形）	quán	2-7
全家福	（名）	quánjiāfú	4-7
拳	（名）	quán	3-10
缺	（动）	quē	3-4
缺点	（名）	quēdiǎn	5-10
却	（副）	què	5-2
确实	（副）	quèshí	5-5
裙子	（名）	qúnzi	3-9
群	（量）	qún	5-8
R			
然后	（连）	ránhòu	3-8
让	（动）	ràng	2-7
让	（介）	ràng	5-8
让座儿	（动）	ràngzuòr	5-6
绕	（动）	rào	5-5
热	（形）	rè	2-3
热乎乎	（形）	rèhūhū	5-1
热闹	（形）	rènao	4-7

热情	（形）	rèqíng	3-3
热心	（形）	rèxīn	5-1
人	（名）	rén	1-3
人家	（代）	rénjia	5-1
人口	（名）	rénkǒu	5-6
人类	（名）	rénlèi	5-5
人们	（名）	rénmen	3-4
人民币	（名）	rénmínbì	2-3
人生	（名）	rénshēng	4-3
认识	（动）	rènshi	1-4
认为	（动）	rènwéi	2-5
认真	（形）	rènzhēn	3-7
日	（名）	rì	2-9
日报	（名）	rìbào	4-2
日记	（名）	rìjì	5-5
日历	（名）	rìlì	3-2
日期	（名）	rìqī	5-3
日子	（名）	rìzi	5-8
容易	（形）	róngyì	1-10
肉	（名）	ròu	4-5
如	（连）	rú	5-3
如果	（连）	rúguǒ	5-3
如意	（动）	rúyì	2-7
软	（形）	ruǎn	5-7
弱	（形）	ruò	5-8
S			
洒	（动）	sǎ	5-4
赛	（动）	sài	3-1
三	（数）	sān	1-1
伞	（名）	sǎn	4-1
散	（动）	sàn	4-2
散步	（动）	sànbù	3-2
嗓子	（名）	sǎngzi	2-9
扫码	（动）	sǎomǎ	4-6

嫂子	（名）	sǎozi	1-9
色	（名）	sè	3-2
沙丁鱼	（名）	shādīngyú	5-6
沙发	（名）	shāfā	3-7
傻	（形）	shǎ	5-1
山	（名）	shān	2-8
山山水水		shānshānshuǐ-shuǐ	4-3
伤	（名、动）	shāng	5-10
商场	（名）	shāngchǎng	3-9
商店	（名）	shāngdiàn	1-6
商贩	（名）	shāngfàn	5-3
商量	（动）	shāngliang	3-8
上	（名）	shàng	1-6
上班	（动）	shàngbān	2-10
上边	（名）	shàngbian	1-6
上课	（动）	shàngkè	2-2
上面	（名）	shàngmiàn	4-2
上网	（动）	shàngwǎng	3-10
上午	（名）	shàngwǔ	2-2
上衣	（名）	shàngyī	3-9
稍	（副）	shāo	4-6
少	（形）	shǎo	2-2
蛇	（名）	shé	4-5
设计	（动、名）	shèjì	4-5
社会	（名）	shèhuì	5-2
摄氏度	（量）	shèshìdù	3-2
谁	（代）	shéi	2-1
身高	（名）	shēngāo	5-1
身上	（名）	shēnshang	3-9
身体	（名）	shēntǐ	1-7
深厚	（形）	shēnhòu	3-10
什么	（代）	shénme	1-4
神圣	（形）	shénshèng	2-5
婶子	（名）	shěnzi	4-7
升	（动）	shēng	5-4
生	（动）	shēng	4-9
生病	（动）	shēngbìng	4-9
生产	（动）	shēngchǎn	3-9
生词	（名）	shēngcí	1-5
生动	（形）	shēngdòng	5-6
生活	（名）	shēnghuó	2-10
生气	（动）	shēngqì	4-4
生日	（名）	shēngrì	2-6
生意	（名）	shēngyi	3-2
生鱼片	（名）	shēngyúpiàn	4-6
声	（名）	shēng	5-6
声调	（名）	shēngdiào	1-10
声音	（名）	shēngyīn	5-6
省	（动）	shěng	5-2
省	（名）	shěng	5-5
失望	（形）	shīwàng	5-1
师傅	（名）	shīfu	3-9
诗	（名）	shī	4-1
诗人	（名）	shīrén	4-1
十	（数）	shí	1-1
十分	（副）	shífēn	3-9
十字路口		shízì lùkǒu	4-9
石（头）	（名）	shí(tou)	5-5
时光	（名）	shíguāng	3-10
时候	（名）	shíhou	1-10
时间	（名）	shíjiān	2-4
时期	（名）	shíqī	5-5
实现	（动）	shíxiàn	4-3
实在	（副、形）	shízài	4-2
食		shí	4-5
食品	（名）	shípǐn	4-3
食堂	（名）	shítáng	1-6
使	（动）	shǐ	3-6

使用	（动）	shǐyòng	5-10
世界	（名）	shìjiè	2-2
世上	（名）	shìshàng	3-10
市	（名）	shì	2-10
市场	（名）	shìchǎng	3-3
市区	（名）	shìqū	2-10
似的	（助）	shìde	5-6
事情	（名）	shìqing	3-8
事儿	（名）	shìr	1-9
事实	（名）	shìshí	5-10
试	（动）	shì	1-10
视频	（名）	shìpín	3-10
是	（动）	shì	1-3
适合	（动）	shìhé	5-6
室		shì	2-4
收	（动）	shōu	3-6
收件人	（名）	shōujiànrén	5-9
收据	（名）	shōujù	3-5
收拾	（动）	shōushi	2-6
手	（名）	shǒu	1-6
手表	（名）	shǒubiǎo	1-6
手机	（名）	shǒujī	1-6
手术	（名）	shǒushù	4-10
手提电脑		shǒutí diànnǎo	3-10
手纸	（名）	shǒuzhǐ	5-10
首	（量）	shǒu	3-10
首先	（副）	shǒuxiān	5-6
寿		shòu	2-7
受	（动）	shòu	3-9
受伤	（动）	shòushāng	5-10
售货员	（名）	shòuhuòyuán	3-9
售票员	（名）	shòupiàoyuán	5-1
瘦	（形）	shòu	5-3
书	（名）	shū	1-6
书包	（名）	shūbāo	5-8
书店	（名）	shūdiàn	1-6
书法	（名）	shūfǎ	4-1
书房	（名）	shūfáng	4-7
书柜	（名）	shūguì	3-7
书架	（名）	shūjià	1-6
书桌	（名）	shūzhuō	3-7
叔叔	（名）	shūshu	4-4
舒服	（形）	shūfu	2-9
输	（动）	shū	4-1
熟	（形）	shú	4-2
属	（动）	shǔ	2-6
数	（动）	shǔ	2-7
树	（名）	shù	4-10
树林	（名）	shùlín	4-10
数		shù	2-7
数码相机	（名）	shùmǎ xiàngjī	5-8
数学	（名）	shùxué	4-8
数字	（名）	shùzì	2-7
刷卡	（动）	shuākǎ	4-6
摔	（动）	shuāi	5-8
帅	（形）	shuài	5-1
双	（形）	shuāng	2-3
水	（名）	shuǐ	2-8
水果	（名）	shuǐguǒ	2-6
水平	（名）	shuǐpíng	3-5
水煮牛肉		shuǐzhǔ niúròu	4-5
睡觉	（动）	shuìjiào	3-1
顺	（介）	shùn	4-9
顺便	（副）	shùnbiàn	2-10
顺利	（形）	shùnlì	2-7
说	（动）	shuō	1-5
说不定	（副）	shuōbudìng	4-4
说法	（名）	shuōfǎ	5-5

硕士	（名）	shuòshì	5-6
司机	（名）	sījī	5-1
丝	（名）	sī	4-6
丝绸	（名）	sīchóu	3-9
私人	（名）	sīrén	3-8
私事	（名）	sīshì	5-2
死	（动）	sǐ	5-7
四	（数）	sì	1-1
四合院儿	（名）	sìhéyuànr	4-7
四世同堂		sì shì tóngtáng	4-7
送	（动）	sòng	2-2
俗话	（名）	súhuà	4-2
速成	（动）	sùchéng	1-8
宿舍	（名）	sùshè	1-7
酸	（形）	suān	4-6
酸辣汤	（名）	suānlàtāng	4-6
算是	（动）	suànshì	4-8
虽然	（连）	suīrán	3-10
随便	（动）	suíbiàn	2-9
随时	（副）	suíshí	5-2
岁	（量）	suì	2-9
岁数	（名）	suìshu	4-7
所	（量）	suǒ	3-6
所	（名）	suǒ	5-1
所以	（连）	suǒyǐ	5-3
所有	（形）	suǒyǒu	4-4
所长	（名）	suǒzhǎng	5-1

T

他	（代）	tā	1-2
她	（代）	tā	1-2
台	（量）	tái	3-8
台阶	（名）	táijiē	5-5
抬	（动）	tái	5-7
太	（副）	tài	1-4
太极拳	（名）	tàijíquán	3-10
太太	（名）	tàitai	3-9
太阳	（名）	tàiyáng	5-4
态度	（名）	tàidu	3-9
谈	（动）	tán	2-1
汤	（名）	tāng	4-6
糖	（名）	táng	4-4
躺	（动）	tǎng	4-7
趟	（量）	tàng	5-8
讨	（动）	tǎo	5-1
讨价还价		tǎojià-huánjià	3-9
套	（量）	tào	3-3
特别	（副）	tèbié	2-5
特色	（名）	tèsè	4-1
特意	（副）	tèyì	5-9
疼	（形）	téng	2-9
腾飞	（动）	téngfēi	5-5
踢	（动）	tī	3-1
提	（动）	tí	3-7
提高	（动）	tígāo	3-10
提前	（动）	tíqián	5-6
体温	（名）	tǐwēn	2-9
体育	（名）	tǐyù	3-1
体育场	（名）	tǐyùchǎng	3-1
体重	（名）	tǐzhòng	4-4
天	（名）	tiān	1-5
天空	（名）	tiānkōng	5-4
天气	（名）	tiānqì	2-10
天使	（名）	tiānshǐ	4-10
添	（动）	tiān	4-9
甜	（形）	tián	4-4
填	（动）	tián	3-8
填写	（动）	tiánxiě	5-9
挑	（动）	tiāo	3-9

条	（量）	tiáo	2-8
条件	（名）	tiáojiàn	3-10
跳舞	（动）	tiàowǔ	3-3
贴	（动）	tiē	3-5
铁路	（名）	tiělù	4-4
厅	（名）	tīng	3-6
听	（动）	tīng	1-10
听	（名）	tīng	4-6
听力	（名）	tīnglì	2-4
听说	（动）	tīngshuō	2-8
听写	（动）	tīngxiě	1-10
停	（动）	tíng	5-3
挺	（副）	tǐng	4-1
通	（动）	tōng	2-9
……通		…tōng	3-5
通知	（名、动）	tōngzhī	2-6
同	（副）	tóng	2-10
同居	（动）	tóngjū	2-10
同学	（名）	tóngxué	1-8
同意	（动）	tóngyì	3-6
统计	（动）	tǒngjì	5-6
统一	（动）	tǒngyī	5-5
痛苦	（形）	tòngkǔ	5-10
偷	（动、副）	tōu	4-4
偷偷	（副）	tōutōu	4-4
头	（名）	tóu	2-9
透	（形）	tòu	5-9
突然	（形）	tūrán	2-10
图	（名）	tú	1-7
图片	（名）	túpiàn	5-5
图书馆	（名）	túshūguǎn	1-7
兔	（名）	tù	2-6
兔子	（名）	tùzi	2-6
团圆	（动）	tuányuán	5-4
推	（动）	tuī	4-8
腿	（名）	tuǐ	5-8
退	（动）	tuì	5-3
W			
娃娃菜	（名）	wáwacài	4-6
袜子	（名）	wàzi	3-6
外	（名）	wài	2-8
外币	（名）	wàibì	3-8
外边	（名）	wàibian	2-8
外国	（名）	wàiguó	3-6
外科	（名）	wàikē	4-10
外面	（名）	wàimiàn	4-2
外套	（名）	wàitào	3-9
外文	（名）	wàiwén	1-8
外语	（名）	wàiyǔ	1-8
弯曲	（形）	wānqū	5-5
丸	（名、量）	wán	3-4
丸药	（名）	wányào	3-4
完	（动）	wán	2-5
完成	（动）	wánchéng	3-7
完全	（副）	wánquán	1-10
玩儿	（动）	wánr	1-8
玩笑	（名）	wánxiào	3-6
晚	（形）	wǎn	3-7
晚报	（名）	wǎnbào	4-2
晚饭	（名）	wǎnfàn	3-1
晚会	（名）	wǎnhuì	2-6
晚上	（名）	wǎnshang	1-5
碗	（名）	wǎn	4-6
万	（数）	wàn	2-7
万事	（名）	wànshì	2-7
万事如意		wànshì-rúyì	2-7
网	（名）	wǎng	3-3
网吧	（名）	wǎngbā	3-10

网购	（动）	wǎnggòu	3-3
网球	（名）	wǎngqiú	4-5
往	（介）	wǎng	3-5
忘	（动）	wàng	3-6
忘记	（动）	wàngjì	3-6
望	（动）	wàng	5-4
微	（形）	wēi	3-10
微风	（名）	wēifēng	3-10
微信	（名）	wēixìn	3-3
围	（动）	wéi	5-5
围绕	（动）	wéirào	5-5
伟大	（形）	wěidà	5-5
伪劣	（形）	wěiliè	4-4
卫生	（名、形）	wèishēng	5-10
卫生纸	（名）	wèishēngzhǐ	5-10
为	（介）	wèi	2-1
为了	（介）	wèile	4-4
为什么		wèi shénme	2-1
位	（量）	wèi	1-8
味道	（名）	wèidao	3-3
味儿	（名）	wèir	5-1
胃	（名）	wèi	4-10
喂	（叹）	wèi	3-1
文化	（名）	wénhuà	2-5
文件	（名）	wénjiàn	3-8
文学	（名）	wénxué	3-5
文章	（名）	wénzhāng	2-6
闻名	（动）	wénmíng	4-5
问	（动）	wèn	1-8
问好	（动）	wènhǎo	5-3
问号	（名）	wènhào	5-5
问候	（动）	wènhòu	3-10
问题	（名）	wèntí	2-5
我	（代）	wǒ	1-2

卧室	（名）	wòshì	4-4
握	（动）	wò	3-5
乌龙茶	（名）	wūlóngchá	2-9
屋	（名）	wū	3-7
屋子	（名）	wūzi	3-7
无轨电车		wúguǐ-diànchē	4-4
五	（数）	wǔ	1-1
午饭	（名）	wǔfàn	3-1
捂	（动）	wǔ	5-8
物理	（名）	wùlǐ	4-8
误会	（动）	wùhuì	2-10
X			
西	（名）	xī	3-1
西餐	（名）	xīcān	3-5
西方	（名）	xīfāng	3-6
西服	（名）	xīfú	3-9
西瓜	（名）	xīgua	2-9
西面	（名）	xīmiàn	4-2
西药	（名）	xīyào	3-4
吸	（动）	xī	4-4
希望	（动）	xīwàng	3-7
稀		xī	4-2
习惯	（动）	xíguàn	2-10
媳妇	（名）	xífu	5-7
洗	（动）	xǐ	2-6
洗衣店	（名）	xǐyīdiàn	3-3
洗澡	（动）	xǐzǎo	3-10
喜	（形）	xǐ	4-4
喜欢	（动）	xǐhuan	2-3
喜糖	（名）	xǐtáng	4-4
戏	（名）	xì	5-7
系	（名）	xì	2-2
系统	（形、名）	xìtǒng	4-1
下	（动）	xià	1-7

下	（名）	xià	2-8
下班	（动）	xiàbān	2-10
下边	（名）	xiàbian	2-8
下课	（动）	xiàkè	1-7
下面	（名）	xiàmiàn	4-2
下午	（名）	xiàwǔ	2-2
夏季	（名）	xiàjì	2-3
夏天	（名）	xiàtiān	2-3
先	（副）	xiān	3-6
先生	（名）	xiānsheng	2-3
鲜	（形）	xiān	4-10
鲜花	（名）	xiānhuā	4-10
现代	（形）	xiàndài	4-1
现金	（名）	xiànjīn	2-3
现在	（名）	xiànzài	2-2
线	（名）	xiàn	5-6
相	（副）	xiāng	3-10
相当	（副）	xiāngdāng	3-9
相亲相爱		xiāngqīn-xiāng'ài	3-10
相信	（动）	xiāngxìn	4-8
香	（形）	xiāng	4-6
香蕉	（名）	xiāngjiāo	5-3
箱子	（名）	xiāngzi	5-7
享福	（动）	xiǎngfú	5-7
想	（动）	xiǎng	1-9
向	（介）	xiàng	3-7
相	（名）	xiàng	2-9
相片儿	（名）	xiàngpiānr	5-6
项链	（名）	xiàngliàn	5-9
象棋	（名）	xiàngqí	5-7
象征	（名）	xiàngzhēng	5-4
像	（动）	xiàng	3-6
小	（形）	xiǎo	1-9
小便	（动、名）	xiǎobiàn	3-4
小吃	（名）	xiǎochī	4-5
小伙子	（名）	xiǎohuǒzi	5-1
小姐	（名）	xiǎojiě	2-4
小时	（名）	xiǎoshí	2-4
小说	（名）	xiǎoshuō	3-3
小偷儿	（名）	xiǎotōur	5-8
小心	（动）	xiǎoxīn	4-9
小学	（名）	xiǎoxué	2-1
孝顺	（动）	xiàoshùn	5-7
孝心	（名）	xiàoxīn	5-7
校	（名）	xiào	2-1
校园	（名）	xiàoyuán	1-7
校长	（名）	xiàozhǎng	2-1
笑	（动）	xiào	2-9
笑话	（动、名）	xiàohua	5-10
些	（量）	xiē	2-8
鞋	（名）	xié	3-3
写	（动）	xiě	1-5
血	（名）	xiě	3-4
泻	（动）	xiè	4-10
谢	（动）	xiè	1-5
心	（名）	xīn	2-7
心爱	（形）	xīn'ài	5-9
心思	（名）	xīnsi	5-8
心想事成		xīnxiǎng-shìchéng	2-7
新	（形）	xīn	2-7
新年	（名）	xīnnián	2-7
新奇	（形）	xīnqí	5-2
新闻	（名）	xīnwén	4-1
信	（名）	xìn	2-1
信	（动）	xìn	4-8
信封	（名）	xìnfēng	5-7
信用卡	（名）	xìnyòngkǎ	5-9
信誉	（名）	xìnyù	5-3

信纸	（名）	xìnzhǐ	5-10
兴奋	（形）	xīngfèn	5-6
星级	（名）	xīngjí	5-7
星期	（名）	xīngqī	2-10
星期日	（名）	xīngqīrì	2-10
星期天	（名）	xīngqītiān	2-10
星星	（名）	xīngxing	5-4
行	（形）	xíng	1-7
行李	（名）	xíngli	4-7
行政区	（名）	xíngzhèngqū	5-5
醒	（动）	xǐng	5-9
兴趣	（名）	xìngqù	2-5
幸福	（形）	xìngfú	2-7
……性		…xìng	4-10
姓	（名、动）	xìng	1-3
休息	（动）	xiūxi	1-7
修	（动）	xiū	2-9
修建	（动）	xiūjiàn	5-5
修理	（动）	xiūlǐ	2-9
需要	（动、名）	xūyào	5-10
许	（动）	xǔ	4-5
许多	（数）	xǔduō	4-3
学	（动）	xué	1-7
学生	（名）	xuésheng	1-8
学术	（名）	xuéshù	5-6
学问	（名）	xuéwen	4-5
学习	（动）	xuéxí	1-7
学校	（名）	xuéxiào	1-8
学院	（名）	xuéyuàn	1-8
雪	（名）	xuě	3-2
雪碧	（名）	xuěbì	4-6
血压	（名）	xuèyā	3-4
训练	（动）	xùnliàn	3-7
驯	（动）	xùn	5-8

Y			
鸭	（名）	yā	4-3
牙	（名）	yá	2-9
呀	（助）	ya	2-2
烟	（名）	yān	4-4
严	（形）	yán	4-8
严格	（形）	yángé	3-7
沿	（介）	yán	4-3
研究	（动）	yánjiū	2-1
研究生	（名）	yánjiūshēng	2-1
颜色	（名）	yánsè	3-9
眼	（名）	yǎn	4-1
眼镜	（名）	yǎnjìng	5-2
眼睛	（名）	yǎnjing	4-1
眼前	（名）	yǎnqián	4-1
演	（动）	yǎn	5-7
演出	（动）	yǎnchū	5-7
羊	（名）	yáng	5-3
养	（动）	yǎng	5-7
养成		yǎngchéng	5-10
样	（量）	yàng	5-9
样儿	（名）	yàngr	2-3
样子	（名）	yàngzi	3-9
要求	（名）	yāoqiú	3-7
邀请	（动）	yāoqǐng	4-2
遥远	（形）	yáoyuǎn	3-10
药	（名）	yào	2-9
药方	（名）	yàofāng	3-4
药片儿	（名）	yàopiànr	3-4
要	（能动）	yào	1-7
要	（连）	yào	2-5
要紧	（形）	yàojǐn	3-4
要命	（动）	yàomìng	4-9
要是	（连）	yàoshi	2-5

要死	（动）	yàosǐ	4-9
钥匙	（名）	yàoshi	4-9
爷爷	（名）	yéye	1-9
也	（副）	yě	1-4
野	（形）	yě	5-8
页	（量）	yè	3-5
夜	（名）	yè	3-4
夜间	（名）	yèjiān	3-2
夜里	（名）	yèli	3-4
夜晚	（名）	yèwǎn	5-4
一	（数）	yī	1-1
一……就……		yī…jiù…	3-4
一……也/都……		yī…yě/dōu…	5-6
衣服	（名）	yīfu	2-3
衣柜	（名）	yīguì	3-7
医院	（名）	yīyuàn	2-1
一半儿	（数）	yíbànr	3-4
一定	（副）	yídìng	1-10
一共	（副）	yígòng	1-4
一会儿	（数量）	yíhuìr	3-8
一块儿	（副）	yíkuàir	4-5
一律	（副）	yílǜ	5-3
一切	（代）	yíqiè	2-7
一下儿	（数量）	yíxiàr	1-8
一样	（形）	yíyàng	1-10
姨	（名）	yí	4-7
姨父	（名）	yífu	4-7
遗产	（名）	yíchǎn	5-5
遗憾	（形）	yíhàn	2-7
已	（副）	yǐ	2-6
已经	（副）	yǐjīng	2-6
以后	（名）	yǐhòu	1-8
以前	（名）	yǐqián	3-1

以上	（名）	yǐshàng	2-3
以为	（动）	yǐwéi	4-4
以下	（名）	yǐxià	2-3
椅子	（名）	yǐzi	3-7
一般	（形）	yìbān	4-8
一边……一边……		yìbiān…yìbiān…	1-10
一点儿	（数量）	yìdiǎnr	2-3
一回生，两回熟		yì huí shēng, liǎng huí shú	4-2
一起	（副）	yìqǐ	1-9
一生	（名）	yìshēng	3-5
一时	（副）	yìshí	5-4
一手儿	（名）	yìshǒur	4-8
一些	（数量）	yìxiē	2-8
一直	（副）	yìzhí	4-2
亿	（数）	yì	3-2
义务	（形）	yìwù	5-1
意见	（名）	yìjiàn	3-7
意思	（名）	yìsi	1-10
因此	（连）	yīncǐ	4-9
因为	（连）	yīnwei	3-4
阴	（形）	yīn	3-2
音频	（名）	yīnpín	3-10
音乐	（名）	yīnyuè	2-6
银	（名）	yín	3-10
银白	（形）	yínbái	5-4
银行	（名）	yínháng	3-8
银婚	（名）	yínhūn	3-10
银子	（名）	yínzi	3-10
饮料	（名）	yǐnliào	2-9
应该	（能动）	yīnggāi	3-5
营业	（动）	yíngyè	2-2
营业员	（名）	yíngyèyuán	2-2
赢	（动）	yíng	4-1

赢得	（动）	yíngdé	4-1
影响	（动、名）	yǐngxiǎng	4-4
哟	（叹）	yō	2-9
拥挤	（形）	yōngjǐ	5-6
永远	（副）	yǒngyuǎn	2-7
用	（动）	yòng	1-10
用功	（形）	yònggōng	3-4
优惠	（形）	yōuhuì	2-3
优良	（形）	yōuliáng	5-1
优美	（形）	yōuměi	4-10
优盘	（名）	yōupán	3-4
优秀	（形）	yōuxiù	5-1
悠久	（形）	yōujiǔ	4-1
由	（介）	yóu	4-1
邮费	（名）	yóufèi	3-5
邮件	（名）	yóujiàn	2-1
邮局	（名）	yóujú	3-5
邮票	（名）	yóupiào	3-5
油	（名）	yóu	5-10
油腻	（形）	yóunì	4-5
游	（动）	yóu	4-3
游览	（动）	yóulǎn	4-3
游泳	（动）	yóuyǒng	3-2
友谊	（名）	yǒuyì	3-1
有	（动）	yǒu	1-5
有的	（代）	yǒude	4-8
有点儿	（副）	yǒudiǎnr	2-10
有害	（形）	yǒuhài	4-4
有名	（形）	yǒumíng	4-3
有时	（副）	yǒushí	3-7
有时候	（副）	yǒushíhou	3-7
有些	（代）	yǒuxiē	5-2
有意思		yǒu yìsi	2-5
有用	（形）	yǒuyòng	3-3

又	（副）	yòu	2-4
又…… 又……		yòu…yòu…	3-3
右	（名）	yòu	2-8
右边	（名）	yòubian	2-8
右面	（名）	yòumiàn	4-2
幼儿	（名）	yòu’ér	2-10
幼儿园	（名）	yòu’éryuán	2-10
于是	（连）	yúshì	3-9
鱼香肉丝		yúxiāng ròusī	4-6
愉快	（形）	yúkuài	5-6
宇航员	（名）	yǔhángyuán	5-5
羽毛球	（名）	yǔmáoqiú	4-5
雨	（名）	yǔ	3-2
语伴儿	（名）	yǔbànr	3-8
语调	（名）	yǔdiào	5-10
语法	（名）	yǔfǎ	2-4
语音	（名）	yǔyīn	1-10
预报	（名）	yùbào	3-2
预订	（动）	yùdìng	2-3
预习	（动）	yùxí	1-7
遇	（动）	yù	1-7
遇到		yùdào	2-10
遇见	（动）	yùjiàn	1-7
元	（量）	yuán	2-3
元宵	（名）	yuánxiāo	5-4
……员		…yuán	3-9
原来	（副）	yuánlái	4-1
原因	（名）	yuányīn	2-5
圆	（形）	yuán	5-4
圆珠笔	（名）	yuánzhūbǐ	2-2
远	（形）	yuǎn	1-9
远在天边，近在眼前		yuǎn zài tiānbiān, jìn zài yǎnqián	4-1

院	（名）	yuàn	4-1
院长	（名）	yuànzhǎng	2-1
院子	（名）	yuànzi	4-7
愿	（能动）	yuàn	3-10
愿望	（名）	yuànwàng	4-3
愿意	（能动）	yuànyì	3-3
约	（动）	yuē	5-9
约会	（名）	yuēhuì	5-9
月	（名）	yuè	3-2
月饼	（名）	yuèbing	5-3
月光	（名）	yuèguāng	5-4
月亮	（名）	yuèliang	5-4
阅读	（动）	yuèdú	3-8
阅览室	（名）	yuèlǎnshì	3-3
越……越……		yuè…yuè…	5-8
云	（名）	yún	3-2
云彩	（名）	yúncai	5-4
允许	（动）	yǔnxǔ	4-5
运	（动）	yùn	3-5
运动	（名）	yùndòng	4-5
运动员	（名）	yùndòngyuán	4-9
		Z	
杂技	（名）	zájì	5-3
杂志	（名）	zázhì	3-5
再	（副）	zài	1-7
再见	（动）	zàijiàn	1-7
再说	（连）	zàishuō	5-3
在	（动）	zài	1-5
在	（副）	zài	4-1
咱们	（代）	zánmen	3-1
攒	（动）	zǎn	5-7
赞扬	（动）	zànyáng	4-1
糟糕	（形）	zāogāo	2-6
早	（形）	zǎo	2-9
早晨	（名）	zǎochen	5-9
早饭	（名）	zǎofàn	3-1
早日	（副）	zǎorì	2-9
早上	（名）	zǎoshang	3-1
造句	（动）	zàojù	1-10
责怪	（动）	zéguài	5-10
怎么	（代）	zěnme	1-10
怎么回事		zěnme huí shì	3-8
怎么样	（代）	zěnmeyàng	1-7
增加	（动）	zēngjiā	4-4
增长	（动）	zēngzhǎng	4-5
展览	（动）	zhǎnlǎn	5-7
战场	（名）	zhànchǎng	5-8
战争	（名）	zhànzhēng	5-8
站	（动）	zhàn	4-7
站	（名）	zhàn	4-9
张	（量）	zhāng	2-2
长	（动）	zhǎng	4-1
掌握	（动）	zhǎngwò	5-10
丈夫	（名）	zhàngfu	3-6
账	（名）	zhàng	4-6
招呼	（动）	zhāohu	5-3
招生	（动）	zhāoshēng	4-1
着	（动）	zháo	3-4
着急	（形）	zháojí	1-6
找	（动）	zhǎo	1-6
照	（动）	zhào	2-9
照顾	（动）	zhàogù	3-9
照片	（名）	zhàopiàn	3-6
照相	（动）	zhàoxiàng	2-9
照相机	（名）	zhàoxiàngjī	5-8
哲学	（名）	zhéxué	5-7
这	（代）	zhè	1-4

这边	（名）	zhèbian	1-5
这里	（代）	zhèli	3-10
这儿	（代）	zhèr	1-6
这些	（代）	zhèxiē	3-3
着	（助）	zhe	3-5
珍贵	（形）	zhēnguì	5-9
珍惜	（动）	zhēnxī	4-2
真	（副）	zhēn	2-4
真	（形）	zhēn	2-10
真实	（形）	zhēnshí	5-10
真正	（形）	zhēnzhèng	5-5
阵	（量）	zhèn	3-10
争取	（动）	zhēngqǔ	4-2
整个	（形）	zhěnggè	5-6
整齐	（形）	zhěngqí	2-6
正	（副）	zhèng	1-10
正常	（形）	zhèngcháng	2-9
正好	（副、形）	zhènghǎo	4-5
正确	（形）	zhèngquè	5-10
正在	（副）	zhèngzài	2-6
证书	（名）	zhèngshū	4-2
政府	（名）	zhèngfǔ	4-5
挣	（动）	zhèng	5-2
……之一		zhī yī	4-5
支	（量）	zhī	2-2
只	（量）	zhī	2-1
枝	（量）	zhī	2-7
知	（动）	zhī	2-2
知道	（动）	zhīdao	2-2
知识	（名）	zhīshi	5-8
值得	（动）	zhíde	3-6
职业	（名）	zhíyè	2-5
职员	（名）	zhíyuán	2-1
止	（动）	zhǐ	4-10

只	（副）	zhǐ	1-9
只好	（副）	zhǐhǎo	5-3
只是	（副）	zhǐshì	2-5
只是	（连）	zhǐshì	3-7
只要……就……		zhǐyào…jiù…	3-5
只有	（连）	zhǐyǒu	3-10
纸	（名）	zhǐ	3-8
质量	（名）	zhìliàng	3-9
治	（动）	zhì	4-6
治疗	（动）	zhìliáo	4-10
中	（形）	zhōng	3-2
中	（名）	zhōng	4-2
中餐	（名）	zhōngcān	3-5
中间	（名）	zhōngjiān	2-9
中午	（名）	zhōngwǔ	3-1
中学	（名）	zhōngxué	2-1
中药	（名）	zhōngyào	3-4
终于	（副）	zhōngyú	5-5
钟	（名）	zhōng	3-1
钟头	（名）	zhōngtóu	5-2
种	（量）	zhǒng	2-2
种	（动）	zhòng	4-9
重	（形）	zhòng	3-5
重量	（名）	zhòngliàng	3-5
重要	（形）	zhòngyào	4-8
周	（名）	zhōu	2-3
周	（量）	zhōu	5-5
周到	（形）	zhōudào	3-6
周围	（名）	zhōuwéi	4-4
猪	（名）	zhū	4-5
猪手	（名）	zhūshǒu	4-5
主意	（名）	<口>zhúyi	2-4
主妇	（名）	zhǔfù	2-1
主讲	（动）	zhǔjiǎng	4-1

主人	（名）	zhǔrén	5-7
主任	（名）	zhǔrèn	2-1
主食	（名）	zhǔshí	4-6
主席	（名）	zhǔxí	3-9
主席台	（名）	zhǔxítái	3-9
主要	（形）	zhǔyào	5-4
煮	（动）	zhǔ	5-7
住	（动）	zhù	1-8
住院	（动）	zhùyuàn	4-9
住址	（名）	zhùzhǐ	2-10
注意	（动）	zhùyì	1-7
祝	（动）	zhù	2-7
祝贺	（动）	zhùhè	4-7
抓紧	（动）	zhuājǐn	4-2
专门	（副、形）	zhuānmén	3-5
专心	（形）	zhuānxīn	3-6
砖	（名）	zhuān	5-5
转	（动）	zhuǎn	3-2
转	（动）	zhuàn	4-4
装	（动）	zhuāng	5-3
壮	（形）	zhuàng	5-8
状况	（名）	zhuàngkuàng	5-6
准	（形）	zhǔn	2-10
准备	（动）	zhǔnbèi	2-5
准确	（形）	zhǔnquè	5-9
准时	（形）	zhǔnshí	2-10
桌	（量）	zhuō	5-7
桌子	（名）	zhuōzi	1-6
滋味	（名）	zīwèi	5-6
子		zǐ	4-8

紫	（形）	zǐ	1-9
自己	（代）	zìjǐ	2-9
自行车	（名）	zìxíngchē	2-8
自由	（形）	zìyóu	3-2
自由泳	（名）	zìyóuyǒng	3-2
字	（名）	zì	3-2
综合	（动）	zōnghé	4-3
综合课	（名）	zōnghékè	4-3
总	（副）	zǒng	5-1
总是	（副）	zǒngshì	5-1
走	（动）	zǒu	1-9
足迹	（名）	zújì	4-3
足球	（名）	zúqiú	3-1
组织	（动）	zǔzhī	5-2
最	（副）	zuì	1-5
最好	（副）	zuìhǎo	2-3
最近	（名）	zuìjìn	1-5
遵守	（动）	zūnshǒu	4-9
昨天	（名）	zuótiān	1-9
左	（名）	zuǒ	2-8
左边	（名）	zuǒbian	2-8
左面	（名）	zuǒmiàn	4-2
作业	（名）	zuòyè	1-5
坐	（动）	zuò	2-7
座	（量）	zuò	2-8
座位	（名）	zuòwèi	5-6
做	（动）	zuò	1-5
做客	（动）	zuòkè	4-2
做梦	（动）	zuòmèng	4-7
做主	（动）	zuòzhǔ	4-8

专名 Proper nouns

A		
阿虎	Ā Hǔ	5-9
阿拉伯文	Ālābówén	2-4
阿拉伯语	Ālābóyǔ	2-4
阿龙	Ā Lóng	5-9
埃及	Āijí	4-3
艾米	Àimǐ	1-2
澳大利亚	Àodàlìyà	4-3
B		
八达岭	Bādá Lǐng	5-5
白华	Bái Huá	1-1
北海	Běihǎi	3-7
北京	Běijīng	2-4
北京大学	Běijīng Dàxué	5-3
北京晚报	Běijīng Wǎnbào	4-2
贝拉	Bèilā	2-1
彼得	Bǐdé	2-5
C		
长城	Chángchéng	4-3
嫦娥	Cháng'é	5-4
嫦娥奔月	Cháng'é bēn yuè	5-4
陈红	Chén Hóng	5-7
陈文山	Chén Wénshān	4-1
川	Chuān	4-5
春节	Chūnjié	5-4
春秋	Chūnqiū	5-5
D		
大连	Dàlián	3-1
大内上子	Dànèi Shàngzǐ	1-2
大洋洲	Dàyángzhōu	4-3
德文	Déwén	2-4
德语	Déyǔ	2-4
丁	Dīng	2-4
丁兰	Dīng Lán	1-9
端午节	Duānwǔjié	5-4
E		
俄文	Éwén	2-4
俄语	Éyǔ	2-4
F		
法文	Fǎwén	2-4
法语	Fǎyǔ	2-4
方龙	Fāng Lóng	1-1
方云天	Fāng Yúntiān	1-8
非洲	Fēizhōu	4-3
复兴门	Fùxīng Mén	4-9
G		
高	Gāo	3-4
高敏	Gāo Mǐn	4-9
高山	Gāo Shān	5-1
高英	Gāo Yīng	4-1
故宫	Gùgōng	4-3
广东	Guǎngdōng	4-5
广州	Guǎngzhōu	3-1
桂林	Guìlín	4-3
H		
哈尔滨	Hā'ěrbīn	5-3
海伦	Hǎilún	2-1
韩国	Hánguó	2-5

苏州	Sūzhōu	3-9
孙	Sūn	3-9
T		
天安门	Tiān'ān Mén	5-5
天津	Tiānjīn	3-1
W		
王才	Wáng Cái	1-7
王欢	Wáng Huān	1-4
吴	Wú	3-9
武汉	Wǔhàn	5-3
X		
西安	Xī'ān	3-1
西班牙文	Xībānyáwén	2-4
西班牙语	Xībānyáyǔ	2-4
西湖	Xī Hú	4-3
西直门	Xīzhí Mén	4-9
香山	Xiāng Shān	3-6
新疆	Xīnjiāng	4-3
Y		
亚洲	Yàzhōu	4-3
杨静	Yáng Jìng	4-7
颐和园	Yíhé Yuán	3-7
意大利	Yìdàlì	2-5
意大利文	Yìdàlìwén	2-4
意大利语	Yìdàlìyǔ	2-4
英汉词典	Yīng-Hàn Cídiǎn	2-2
英文	Yīngwén	2-4
英语	Yīngyǔ	2-4
于	Yú	2-4
元宵节	Yuánxiāojié	5-4
Z		
张	Zhāng	2-4
赵	Zhào	2-4
赵林	Zhào Lín	2-10
郑	Zhèng	3-9
支付宝	Zhīfùbǎo	2-3
中国	Zhōngguó	1-4
《中国民俗研究》	《Zhōngguó Mínsú Yánjiū》	5-2
《中国文化研究》	《Zhōngguó Wénhuà Yánjiū》	3-6
中秋节	Zhōngqiūjié	5-3
中文	Zhōngwén	1-6
周	Zhōu	3-9
周小芳	Zhōu Xiǎofāng	5-1

Key to exercises and homework
课堂练习和家庭作业参考答案

第一课

三、课堂练习

（二）词语

从本课生词表中选择合适的词语填空

（1）今天早上我在小吃店吃了一个炸糕/包子/粽子，两根油条和一碗馄饨。

（2）12月31日晚上，学校举行新年招待会，邀请各国留学生参加。

（3）这件小礼物不太贵，可是做得非常精致。

（4）你喜欢吃猪肉馅儿的饺子还是羊肉馅儿的？

（5）馄饨跟饺子不一样。

（6）孙小英嫁给了彼得的哥哥。

（7）我告诉你一个好消息，你这次考试成绩全班第一。

（8）这是一个秘密，她谁也不告诉。

（9）他买了一份快餐，吃完以后马上去教室了。

（10）这个地区的人喜欢吃咸的，做什么菜都放很多盐或者酱油。

（11）这个商店卖的西服有很多种类，你可以任意选择。

（12）我计划明年夏天再来这里进修。

（13）这两个句子有什么不同/区别？

（14）中国人常常用茶来招待客人。

（15）四川口味的菜很辣，你能吃吗？

（16）这两篇文章内容相同，肯定是一个人写的。

（17）春天到了，公园里开满了各种各样的鲜花。

（18）明天你有什么安排吗？

（19）这个菜色、香、味、形俱佳。

（20）端午节那天，方老师送给我们每人一个粽子。

（21）你的文章题目是什么？

（22）他们听到这个消息马上行动起来。

（23）请问，买去上海的火车票在哪儿排队？

（24）昨天看京剧我坐在第五排。

（25）请大家排队上车。

（三）句型

2. 用括号里的词语改写下列句子

（1）你喜欢什么我喜欢什么。

（2）你买什么词典我买什么词典。

（3）你买几本我买几本。

（4）你换多少美元我换多少美元。

（5）你邀请谁我邀请谁。

（6）你邀请哪些人我邀请哪些人。

（7）你去哪儿我去哪儿。

（8）你怎么去我怎么去。

（9）你在哪儿复习我在哪儿复习。

（10）你在什么地方复习我在什么地方复习。

（11）谁都帮助过我。

（12）哪儿我都想去。

（13）怎么去都行。

（14）哪天去都可以。

（15）这些小吃哪种我都没吃过。

（16）这些小吃我什么都没吃过。

（17）题目哪个都很难写。

第二课

三、课堂练习

（二）词语

从本课生词表中选择合适的词语填空

（1）这个湖，南边比较浅，北边有的地方非常深。

（2）我不想买白色的，给我拿一件深颜色的试试。

（3）她从钱包里掏出100元。

（4）我跟他说话，可是他不理我。

（5）淘宝、京东是中国人最常用的网上购物平台。

（6）司机打开空调后，让我把车窗关上。

（7）车开之后请不要把头伸出车外。

（8）我的心情像湖水一样平静。

（9）我对这件事儿一点儿印象也没有，都忘光了。

（10）开始上课的时候，你们给老师鞠躬吗？

（11）孩子上学前，父母要教会他们自己穿衣服、系鞋带。

（12）那个商店的售货员说话和气，我喜欢去那儿买东西。

（13）那个孩子没有礼貌，从来不跟别人打招呼。

（14）小王今天显得很高兴，一定遇到了什么好事儿。

（15）那种动物从地球上永远地消失了。

（16）小刘今天有约会，穿得非常时髦。

（17）我们大学毕业以后已经20年没有联系了，我不知道他现在在哪儿。

（18）我们国家的大使馆举行招待会，邀请孙校长参加。

（19）你赶快走！他们在外边等你呢。

（20）公园里开满了各种颜色的花儿，有红的、黄的、紫的、浅蓝的，好看极了。

（21）突然，一个粗重的男声叫了起来：“小心汽车！”

（22）一个黑头发大眼睛的姑娘微笑着说：“见到您很高兴。”

第三课

三、课堂练习

（二）词语

从本课生词表中选择合适的词语填空

（1）北京是中国的首都。

（2）这里的风景真美。

（3）我们学校有很多著名的教授。

（4）这条小河从山上流下来，河水真清。

（5）贝拉白皮肤，蓝眼睛，黄头发，一看就知道是欧洲姑娘。

（6）明天我无论如何都要去医院看看张老师。

（7）小孙昨天刚从国外/家乡回来，今天就开始工作了。

（8）这件事使我回忆起小时候的一件事。

（9）这个城市有很多工人失业了，他们的生活很困难。

（10）站在我家的阳台上可以看见西山。

（11）他说的家乡是指老家，不是这里的家。

（12）他用手指了一下自己，又指了一下外边，意思是他想去外边。

（13）你昨天说去，今天又说不去，你究竟去不去？

（14）学校外边有一个书店可以租书，一本书一天一块钱。

（15）他们全家从一个大城市迁居到这个小镇来了。

（16）这个商店不仅服务态度好，而且物价便宜。

（17）他不是不会，而是粗心，所以这道题又做错了。

（18）不是因为她的身材不苗条，而是因为衣服大小不合适。

（19）这个建筑是哪个朝代修建的，谁也不知道。

（20）我身上仅有10块钱了。

第四课

三、课堂练习

（二）词语

从本课生词表中选择合适的词语填空

（1）小黄经常照顾这个无儿无女的老人。

（2）对你们的帮助我表示衷心的感谢。

（3）你吃不了一个面包，分给我一半儿吧。

（4）那个姑娘在衣服上绣了一朵花。

（5）海员们在船上工作，他们非常辛苦。

（6）你看，门上挂着“请勿打扰/打搅”的牌子，彼得可能睡觉了。

（7）这几天他总是打扰/打搅我，真受不了。

（8）我父亲的脾气不好，他常常跟母亲发脾气。

（9）这个小镇上每家每户都买了小汽车。

（10）你怎么不问问价钱就买？你又上当了。

（11）今天我在路上看见一辆汽车轧伤了一个小孩儿。

（12）下个月有个重要的国际会议在我们大学召开。

（13）我从小时候就喜欢劳动，常常帮助父母干活儿。

（14）感觉这张彩色照片没有那张黑白的效果好。

（15）我刚要给王才打电话，正巧他来了。

（16）这种药治感冒效果不错，我吃了三片儿就好了。

（17）我们班的老师都很有经验，教学效果非常好。

（18）我的脚在踢球的时候受了伤。

（19）你要是热就把衣服脱了吧。

（20）你的这种态度说明你不喜欢他。

（21）教师是做教育工作的人。

（22）我们当天就知道了考试成绩。

四、家庭作业

（一）词语

2. 用括号里的词语改写句子

（1）谁都喜欢他的表演。

（2）谁都不喜欢战争。/没有谁喜欢战争。

（3）谁都不愿意参加她的生日晚会。/没有谁愿意参加她的生日晚会。

（4）谁都讨厌他。

（5）明天你哪儿也不能去。

（6）这种丝绸哪儿也买不到。

（7）你什么时候来我都欢迎。

（8）你什么东西也不要买。

（9）他什么会议都不参加。

（10）他什么事情都不害怕。

（二）阅读

1. 看第一遍后选择正确答案

（1）A （2）B （3）B （4）A

第五课

三、课堂练习

（二）词语

1. 从本课生词表中选择合适的词语填空

（1）小张真了不起，他在运动会上得了四个第一。

（2）今天是我22周岁生日。

(3) 您贵姓？怎么称呼？

(4) 王欢的妻子是中学的语文老师。

(5) 京剧是中国的传统艺术。

(6) 小王喜欢艺术，他以后希望成为一名电影演员。

(7) 方老师非常孝顺他的父母，是个难得的好人。

(8) 喜欢帮助别人是一种高尚的精神。

(9) 文学要反映新时代的新思想。

(10) 我和彼得同时到达北京。

(11) 考试可以检查学生的学习情况，同时也检查老师教的情况。

(12) 大家都尊敬道德高尚的人。

(13) 老师和学生都非常重视这次考试。

(14) 你们有很大的进步，希望你们继续努力，达到更高的水平。

(15) 我真后悔当时没听父母的话。

(16) 时间快到了，赶紧走吧。

(17) 自从前年他去了法国，至今没给我打过电话。

(18) 小时候的朋友很久没有联系，现在都生分了。

(19) 他说了几句笑话，气氛一下子缓和下来了。

(20) 我们爱好和平，反对战争。

(21) 这个地区人民的生活已经达到了小康水平。

(22) 我们都盼望收到亲人的来信。

(23) 这个房间太乱了，咱们收拾一下吧。

(24) 孩子都一周岁了，还没给他起名儿。

第六课

三、课堂练习

（二）词语

1. 连线并朗读

一条	胡同
引起	兴趣
有关	单位
排列	整齐
文化	遗产
风俗	奇特
内容	丰富
亲自	参加
新鲜	空气
主要	人物
旅游	项目
呼吸	困难

2. 从本课生词表中选择合适的词语填空

（1）这个城市的街道没有北京的宽，都很窄。

（2）小刘说的问题很重要，引起了大家的注意。

（3）北京胡同的数目太多了，很难数清楚。

（4）我们还邀请了学校的有关领导参加今天的晚会。

（5）这条胡同是以一个历史人物的名字命名的。

（6）白老师做的面条儿细似头发。

（7）外面下起了牛毛细雨。

（8）这本小说记录了这个城市的变迁。

（9）这个班里充满了浓厚的学习气氛。

（10）陈平想当电视节目主持人。

（11）你说得太夸张了！面条儿怎么可能像头发那么细？

（12）你的衣服脏了，脱下来洗洗吧。

（13）近现代很多著名的历史人物都出自湖南省。

（14）这篇文章的内容非常丰富。

（15）那个病人呼吸越来越困难了。

（16）马校长亲自把我们送到火车站。

（17）我对体育不感兴趣，什么运动项目也没参加。

（18）这些水果很新鲜，也不太贵。

（19）网络在人民生活中起着越来越大的作用。

（20）这个城市应该改造交通，加宽街道，修建立交桥。

（三）句型

2. 选择正确的回答

（1）d　（2）g　（3）c　（4）a

（5）f　（6）b　（7）e　（8）h

第七课

三、课堂练习

（二）词语

1. 连线并朗读

左列	右列
茉莉	水面
饮茶	幸福
上等	花茶
享受	福建
浮在	专家
产于	艺术家
解	矿泉水
多种	节目
洽谈	功能
交流	生意
人民	毒
曲艺	信息

（连线：茉莉—花茶；饮茶—专家；上等—矿泉水；享受—幸福；浮在—水面；产于—福建；解—毒；多种—功能；洽谈—生意；交流—信息；人民—艺术家；曲艺—节目）

2. 从本课生词表中选择合适的词语填空

（1）我们的校长是一位教育<u>专家</u>。

（2）黄山毛峰是<u>上等</u>绿茶。

（3）这里的风景<u>简直</u>太美了。

（4）饭后吃水果可以帮助<u>消化</u>。

（5）我最喜欢大熊猫，<u>其次</u>是猴子。

（6）饭后听听音乐是人生的一大<u>享受</u>。

（7）维生素C是人体不可<u>缺少</u>的。

（8）公园是人们休息的<u>场所</u>。

（9）这台电脑有多种<u>功能</u>。

（10）水面上浮着一只小船。

（11）汉语里很多名称是音译的，例如“可口可乐”“沙发”等。

（12）他们的产品大部分出口国外。

（13）他正在跟客人洽谈生意。

（14）牧民们生活在大草原上，他们喜欢喝奶茶。

（15）在中国常能看到孩子们给国旗敬礼。

（16）我很喜欢看曲艺节目。

（17）老师们常常交流教学经验。

（18）这壶茶是刚沏的。

四、家庭作业

（二）阅读

1. 选出课文中没提到的内容

（1）C　（2）B　（3）D　（4）D

第八课

三、课堂练习

（二）词语

1. 连线并朗读

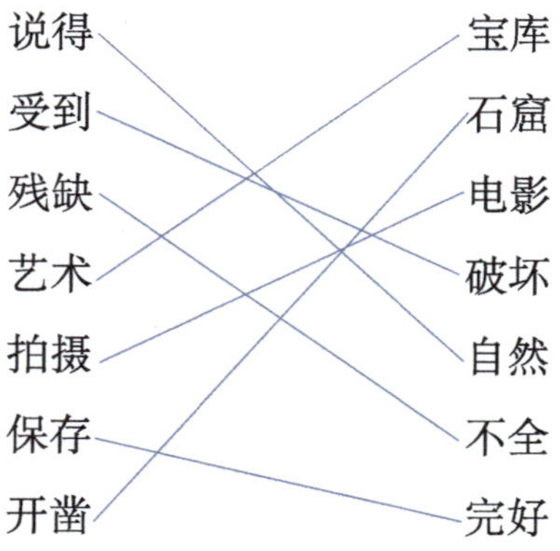

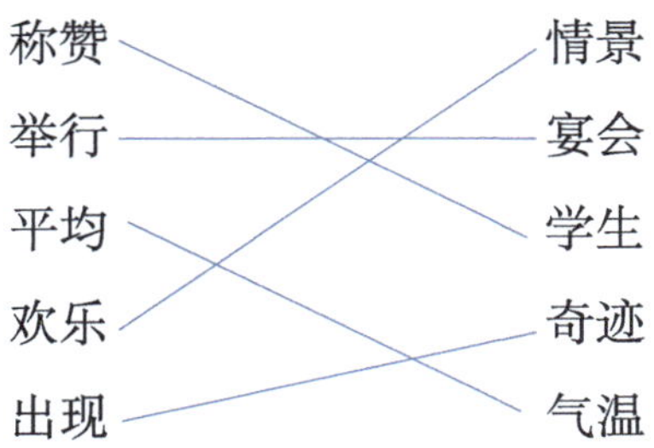

2. 从本课生词表中选择合适的词语填空

（1）这个故事发生在公元10世纪。

（2）最近电视上出现了一些新的主持人。

（3）这条河长约10公里。

（4）这个国家是去年成立的。

（5）你拍照的技术怎么样？

（6）工人们正在开凿山洞，修建铁路。

（7）这些佛像残缺不全了，好像是人为破坏的。

（8）大内从小喜欢美术，她画的画儿可好看了。

（9）看了山本拍摄的照片，大家都称赞他的拍照技术。

（10）我们班同学的平均年龄是23岁。

（11）人们都很重视保护这些著名的文化遗产。

（12）中国大使馆举行了一个宴会庆祝国庆节。

（13）晚会上同学们有的弹琴，有的唱歌。

（14）你打算在这儿待几天？

（15）我常常想起第一次离开家的情景。

（16）孩子们把腿埋在沙子里。

（17）孩子太小，需要母亲的保护。

（18）老师把考试的要求说得很仔细。

（19）你的发音部位和发音方法不对。

（20）在国庆假期几天里大家都过得很快乐，偏偏只有彼得不高兴。

第九课

三、课堂练习

（二）词语

1. 连线并朗读

请示	实践
坚持	时间
集合	领导
语言	痛快
友好	劳动
体育	出差
心里	相处
办事儿	活动
去南方	科学
学习	同意
请求	电话
急救	拖拉

2. 从本课生词表中选择合适的词语填空

（1）他心情不好的时候总喜欢一个人听歌。

（2）昨天夜里我失眠了，今天有点儿头疼。

（3）这件事儿你能做主吗？要不要请示领导？

（4）今天跟你们一起聊天儿，聊得真痛快！

（5）你们别吵了，我心里烦着呢。

（6）老张去年是科长，今年升处长了。

（7）你有什么心事？能告诉我吗？

（8）我在街上碰见了一个老朋友。

（9）谁是这儿的负责人？

（10）上星期你去哪儿出差了？

（11）如果这个问题解决了，其他问题就好办了。

（12）请你提醒王才，明天下午两点在学校西门集合。

（13）这儿危险！你们别过来。

（14）请你原谅，我把时间记错了。

（15）你的意见是错误的，不要坚持了。

（16）我想利用这次旅行的机会多了解了解中国的民俗。

（17）大夫说我得了肺炎/神经病/精神病。

（18）我的房东是中国人。

（19）他说的趣闻真有意思。

（20）汉语节目表演是语言实践活动。

（21）中国和日本是一衣带水的邻居。

（22）艾米从小爱好文艺，什么唱歌、跳舞、弹琴她都喜欢。

（23）这个病人幸亏送得及时。

（24）他的爱好非常广泛。

（25）这是我一生中难以忘怀的事。

第十课

三、课堂练习

（二）词语

1. 连线并朗读

传	美满
受到	歌曲
生活	栏目
点播	晚归
实时	喜爱
收听	坦率
早出	钱
为人	同学
干涉	车
全体	新闻
赚	吻
撞	别人
热烈的	礼物

2. 从本课生词表中选择合适的词语填空

（1）彼得特别喜爱小动物，他常常去动物园玩儿。

（2）我非常珍惜我们的感情。

（3）我真诚地希望爸爸妈妈健康长寿。

（4）这个城市的交通路况给我留下了很深的印象。

（5）来中国后他很快就认识了很多朋友，并且有了新的生活和工作圈子。

（6）今天是我的生日，我的男朋友在电台为我点播了一首歌曲。

（7）这里的人民过着幸福美满的生活。

(8) 他同时收到了两所大学的录取通知书。

(9) 中国有句老话：一分辛劳，一分收获。

(10) 这件事情最重要，一定要搞好。

(11) 那位老演员的表演感情丰富，给我留下了很深的印象。

(12) 他坦率地说出自己的看法。

(13) 请不要干涉别人的感情生活。

(14) 故宫里的每个宫殿都有自己的故事。

(15) 万一明天下雨，我们还去参观吗？

(16) 30多年后再次见面，让两位老人热泪盈眶。

(17) 在中国，让孩子有一个无忧无虑的童年就是父母的幸福。

(18) 只有下大本钱，才能赚更多的钱。

(19) 他们国家规定，银行存钱产生的利息不上税。

(20) 现在银行的利息减少了。

(21) 大内昨天没做作业，她今天补上了。

(22) 我的钱花光了，得去银行取钱了。

(23) 他英语说得真棒！

(24) 在这个城市，一些人很富，有楼房和汽车；一些人很穷，连饭也吃不饱。

四、家庭作业

（二）阅读

1. 下面哪些是玛丽的想法和做法？（在句子后面括号内打“√”或“×”）

(1) ×　(2) √　(3) √　(4) ×

(5) √　(6) ×　(7) √　(8) √

Index of grammar (Volume 2-Volume 6)
语法索引（第2册—第6册）